CANDIDE

Other titles in the Greenhaven Press Literary Companion Series:

WORLD AUTHORS

Fyodor Dostoyevsky
Homer
Sophocles

WORLD LITERATURE

All Quiet on the Western
  Front
Antigone
Crime and Punishment
Cry, the Beloved Country
Cyrano de Bergerac
The Diary of a Young Girl
A Doll's House
Medea
Night
One Day in the Life of
  Ivan Denisovich
The Stranger

THE GREENHAVEN PRESS
Literary Companion
TO WORLD LITERATURE

READINGS ON

CANDIDE

Thomas Walsh, *Book Editor*

David L. Bender, *Publisher*
Bruno Leone, *Executive Editor*
Bonnie Szumski, *Series Editor*

Greenhaven Press, Inc., San Diego, CA

Every effort has been made to trace the owners of copy-righted material. The articles in this volume may have been edited for content, length, and/or reading level. The titles have been changed to enhance the editorial purpose. Those interested in locating the original source will find the complete citation on the first page of each article.

Library of Congress Cataloging-in-Publication Data

Readings on Candide / editor, Thomas Walsh.
      p. cm. — (The Greenhaven Press literary
companion to world literature)
    Includes bibliographical references and index.
    ISBN 0-7377-0361-X (pbk. : alk. paper) —
ISBN 0-7377-0362-8 (lib. : alk. paper)
    1. Voltaire, 1694–1778. Candide. I. Title: Candide.
II. Walsh, Thomas, 1960–   . III. Series

PQ2082.C4 R43 2001
843'.5—dc21

                                                  00-024496

Cover photo: Archive Photos

"The world is whatever it is capable of being. Life is neither very good nor very evil. It is tolerable since, generally speaking, people find it so. . . . We must accept life, nature, and her conditions, utilizing them as best we can."

—Voltaire

CONTENTS

Foreword   9

Introduction   11

Voltaire: A Biography   13

Characters and Plot   25

Chapter 1: Attacking *L'Optimisme*

1. Searching for Optimism in a Cruel World
by Roger Pearson   33
Voltaire explores the human desire and need to maintain
order in life, and shows why people have cause for
optimism in their lives.

2. Using Characters to Disprove Optimism
by Haydn Mason   39
Though Voltaire strongly refutes the Optimists' claims that
this is the best of all possible worlds, he says that people
can expect some good things in life.

**3. Voltaire's Attack on Optimism Has a
Humanitarian Goal** *by Virgil W. Topazio*   47
In attacking Optimism, Voltaire tries to raise the reader's level
of awareness concerning the evil and injustice in the world.

Chapter 2: Eldorado and the Gardens in *Candide*

1. The Symbols of the River and the Garden
by Manfred Kusch   57
The perfection of Eldorado is flawed by its stagnation, a
condition Voltaire contrasts to the flowing river that brings
Candide and Cacambo to this "Garden of Eden."

2. Eldorado as an "Impossible Dream"
by Donna Isaacs Dalnekoff   64
Though it is an ideal society, Voltaire understands that the
standards of Eldorado are unattainable.

3. **Eldorado as a Vision of a Better World**
   by David Williams   72
   In Eldorado, Voltaire presents an ideal community that
   gives people hope for a better world.

4. **A Garden of Hope** *by William F. Bottiglia*   81
   Candide's garden community is a model society, showing
   how people can live productively and contentedly.

5. **Mythical and Symbolic Gardens**
   by Patrick Henry   88
   While two "gardens" in Candide are mythical and metaphor-
   ical in nature, a third is strictly symbolic. Each represents a
   stage in Candide's progress from innocence to maturity.

Chapter 3: The Artistry of the Narrative

1. **Using Irony as a Form of Satire**
   by George R. Havens   98
   Voltaire uses several different ironic methods in form and
   language to satirize human foibles and social institutions.

2. **Using Low Comedy to Mock Philosophic
   Pretensions** *by Clifton Cherpak*   105
   Voltaire's burlesque tale is a satire of grand philosophical
   systems that fail to recognize that the world is generally absurd.

3. **Voltaire's Black Humor** *by Alan R. Pratt*   112
   Voltaire's use of black humor to juxtapose the comic and
   the tragic in *Candide* has had a strong influence on many
   contemporary authors.

4. **Playing on His Readers' Desires**
   by Gail S. Reed   121
   Voltaire uses his narrative structure and the effects of evil
   on his characters to involve the readers' own desires and
   expectations in Candide's travails.

Chapter 4: Human Nature as Seen in Voltaire's Characters

1. **Women's Equality in *Candide*** *by Arthur Scherr*   129
   Voltaire's female characters are equal, if not superior, to their
   male counterparts, a reflection, Scherr claims, of Voltaire's "belief in equality and reciprocity between the sexes."

2. **Candide the "Dunce-king"—Exploring Evil Through a Band of Fools** *by Roy S. Wolper*   141
The connection between stupidity and evil is a strong one, and Voltaire explores the ties through his not-so-bright characters.

3. **Voltaire's View of Degenerate Man** *by A. Owen Aldridge*   151
Voltaire examines the degeneration of humans and their corruption of nature, both of which come as a result of boredom and the failure to search out positive methods of doing good.

Chronology   159

For Further Research   164

Index   166

FOREWORD

*"'Tis the good reader that
makes the good book."*

Ralph Waldo Emerson

The story's bare facts are simple: The captain, an old and scarred seafarer, walks with a peg leg made of whale ivory. He relentlessly drives his crew to hunt the world's oceans for the great white whale that crippled him. After a long search, the ship encounters the whale and a fierce battle ensues. Finally the captain drives his harpoon into the whale, but the harpoon line catches the captain about the neck and drags him to his death.

A simple story, a straightforward plot—yet, since the 1851 publication of Herman Melville's *Moby-Dick*, readers and critics have found many meanings in the struggle between Captain Ahab and the whale. To some, the novel is a cautionary tale that depicts how Ahab's obsession with revenge leads to his insanity and death. Others believe that the whale represents the unknowable secrets of the universe and that Ahab is a tragic hero who dares to challenge fate by attempting to discover this knowledge. Perhaps Melville intended Ahab as a criticism of Americans' tendency to become involved in well-intentioned but irrational causes. Or did Melville model Ahab after himself, letting his fictional character express his anger at what he perceived as a cruel and distant god?

Although literary critics disagree over the meaning of *Moby-Dick*, readers do not need to choose one particular interpretation in order to gain an understanding of Melville's novel. Instead, by examining various analyses, they can gain

numerous insights into the issues that lie under the surface
of the basic plot. Studying the writings of literary critics can
also aid readers in making their own assessments of *Moby-
Dick* and other literary works and in developing analytical
thinking skills.

The Greenhaven Literary Companion Series was created
with these goals in mind. Designed for young adults, this
unique anthology series provides an engaging and comprehensive introduction to literary analysis and criticism. The
essays included in the Literary Companion Series are chosen
for their accessibility to a young adult audience and are ex-
pertly edited in consideration of both the reading and com-
prehension levels of this audience. In addition, each essay is
introduced by a concise summation that presents the contributing writer's main themes and insights. Every anthology
in the Literary Companion Series contains a varied selection
of critical essays that cover a wide time span and express diverse views. Wherever possible, primary sources are represented through excerpts from authors' notebooks, letters, and
journals and through contemporary criticism.

Each title in the Literary Companion Series pays careful
consideration to the historical context of the particular author
or literary work. In-depth biographies and detailed chronolo-
gies reveal important aspects of authors' lives and emphasize
the historical events and social milieu that influenced their
writings. To facilitate further research, every anthology in-
cludes primary and secondary source bibliographies of articles and/or books selected for their suitability for young adults.
These engaging features make the Greenhaven Literary Companion series ideal for introducing students to literary analysis in the classroom or as a library resource for young adults
researching the world's great authors and literature.

Exceptional in its focus on young adults, the Greenhaven
Literary Companion Series strives to present literary criticism in a compelling and accessible format. Every title in the
series is intended to spark readers' interest in leading American and world authors, to help them broaden their understanding of literature, and to encourage them to formulate
their own analyses of the literary works that they read. It is
the editors' hope that young adult readers will find these an-
thologies to be true companions in their study of literature.

INTRODUCTION

It is a fascinating irony that Voltaire's greatest legacy is a short novel that does not even reach a hundred pages in most of its published formats. Voltaire's surviving literary output, according to critic Theodore Besterman, approaches 15 million written words, "enough to make twenty Bibles." The irony lies in the fact that Voltaire "took a dim view of prose fiction in general," according to Clifton Cherpak, and he had a habit of "applying the generic term novel to works that he detested."

Voltaire himself probably would love the irony that *Candide* has thrived over the years while his other works have sunk into obscurity, read almost exclusively by graduate students and scholars. And he would almost certainly be proud that his attack on Optimism—a simplistic philosophy that claims that all is as it should be—continues to entertain and teach.

We all can learn a great deal from Voltaire's *Candide.* It is still widely read in high schools and colleges because it deftly interweaves philosophy, satire, humor, and human nature. It is a tale presented by a man who had an incredible eye for behavior and who, with this work, saw everything come together in a flawless narrative. The characters are parodies, but they are not so far removed from reality that readers cannot relate to them or their experiences.

Candide has survived because of its unflagging realism and incredibly adept satire. Voltaire ignored no evils committed by human beings; he turned his back on no transgressions. How can it be that "all is well," as Pangloss claims and Candide parrots for a time, when people die horrible deaths in wars, when outlaws brutalize and murder and rape, when natural disasters level entire cities, killing thousands in mere moments? This is a fundamental question that everyone confronts, and Voltaire answers it quite simply: All is not well.

But this fact does not mean that people cannot find happiness or purpose in their own lives. George R. Havens claims that "*Candide* points out the rubbish and bids us get broom and pick and shovel and fall to work." As Candide concludes at the end of the novel, we must cultivate our gardens—our lives and our immediate surroundings—in order to avoid boredom and vice.

In this literary companion, critics and scholars examine Voltaire's attack on optimism, his use of gardens as metaphors and symbols, his use of narrative style and language, and his examination of human nature and evil. While *Candide* is a short, easy-to-read book, its pages are full of philosophical ideas and literary devices that create what many consider to be a perfect work, one that has kept audiences entertained and critics busy for well over two hundred years.

Candide is certainly an exceptional book. Literary critic Patrick Henry, in his essay "The Modernity of *Candide*" from *Approaches to Teaching Voltaire's "Candide,"* writes that Voltaire's works do "not appeal to modern sensibility; his literary reputation has declined. His poetry, with its paucity of images, and his plays, pale imitations of the great neoclassical tragedies, simply do not excite twentieth-century readers. . . . And yet *Candide* lives on, and it survives alone."

VOLTAIRE: A BIOGRAPHY

The eventful life of François-Marie Arouet—Voltaire, as he renamed himself—did justice and honor to his philosophies. Not surprisingly, it was a life also filled with conflict, as Voltaire spent his early years satirizing and mocking others, before turning in his later years to humanitarian causes. Two stays in prison and several forced exiles from his home city of Paris attest to Voltaire's penchant for getting himself into trouble with the wrong people, though the conflict hardly defines his life.

VOLTAIRE'S CHILDHOOD

Arouet was born to Marie-Marguerite Daumard and François Arouet, a Parisian notary, on November 21, 1694. The family was bourgeois, though his mother's family had recently been elevated to the lesser nobility. Voltaire was the youngest of three children. He was a sickly child, but proved to be extremely precocious with an impressive intelligence and wit. He loved his sister, Marguerite-Catherine, who was nine years older than he. His brother, Armand, of whom he was less fond, was ten years his senior. In later years, Armand grew to be a religious bigot, having adopted extreme views learned at seminary.

Voltaire's mother died when he was seven. When he was ten, Voltaire's father sent him to Louis-le-Grand, a boarding school run by Jesuit priests. Though his father was not a nobleman, he knew that at the school his son would meet the children of nobility and make friendships that could benefit him later in life. The young Voltaire spent seven years at the school, showing a great talent for poetry, history, and theater, and receiving a solid education in the Greek and Latin classic authors, including Cicero, Horace, and Virgil. As a student he excelled, though he later claimed that he learned "Latin and nonsense," and "not a word of Mathematics or of sound philosophy."[1] The school was quite unsuccessful in establishing religious conviction in him as well; in later years he became an ideological foe of the Jesuits as a religious order, though he still admired their love of learning and dedication to teaching.

Voltaire, an engaging youth, cultivated admirers and learned at an early age to appreciate the finer things in life and to aspire to greater social standing. During these years at school his godfather, the abbé de Châteauneuf, took an interest in the boy and his education. The abbé (a title of respect for secular clergy) introduced Voltaire to a group of freethinkers called the Society of the Temple, and Voltaire was at once drawn to the members of the group and their way of life. These men were role models whose influence on the young boy would endure; they attempted to live life to the fullest, focusing on the present and leaving the past behind, while not worrying about the future. They encouraged his poetry and helped him develop a taste and appreciation for the finer things in life, especially food and poetry.

His godfather also introduced him to the elderly courtesan Ninon de l'Enclos, who found him to be so delightful a young man that when she died, she left him two thousand francs, a large sum at the time, with which to buy books.

DECIDING ON A DIRECTION

When he finished school, Voltaire planned on pursuing a life in literature as a man of letters. His father opposed that plan and unsuccessfully tried to convince him to work in law, then sent him to The Hague, Holland, to work as a page in the service of the new French ambassador. This job was cut short rather quickly, though, when Voltaire began an affair with Olympe Dunoyer, or Pimpette. Pimpette was his first love, and he wrote her long, passionate letters and poems. Unfortunately, Voltaire was a penniless nineteen-year-old, and Pimpette's mother was the editor of a society magazine called the *Quintessence.* When the ambassador found out about the affair, he decided to send the young man back to France, as Madame Dunoyer could do a great deal of damage to the ambassador's career in the pages of her magazine. Voltaire's seeming predisposition to conflict was reflected even in his choice of girlfriends.

He returned home to Paris to study law but spent more time writing poetry and going out with friends than he did studying. He was determined to establish a literary reputation, which he knew would bring fame, fortune, and social standing. Unfortunately, one of his greatest talents was satire, and he began to practice this art, ridiculing almost everyone in Parisian society. Though many people were amused by his wit, many others were offended, and he soon had offended the judge of a poetry contest—which he did not win—so strongly that he was advised to leave Paris for a time.

This period of exile he passed as a guest of Monsieur de Caumartin, marquis de St. Ange, at Fontainebleau, a villa just southeast of Paris. Monsieur de Caumartin had a great love for and knowledge of history, which he shared with Voltaire during his stay, especially concerning Henry IV and Louis XIV, both of whom later became the subjects of important books by Voltaire. Though his situation—catered to by intelligent, sophisticated people on a beautiful estate—was ideal, Voltaire was discontented, and longed to return to Paris. There was no name to be made on a country estate; fame awaited him in the capital, if it awaited anywhere.

Soon he returned to Paris and its high style, and to his poetry and satire. Paris of 1715 was the perfect environment for him. Louis XIV had recently died, and an atmosphere of reduced censorship and authority prevailed; religion suffered and satire thrived. The acting head of state, Philip, duke of Orleans—appointed as regent for the five-year-old Louis XV, who was heir to the throne—led a depraved lifestyle. But even in this lax environment Voltaire would pay the penalty for his unchecked wit. He was exiled once more, accused of having written a poem that depicted the regent as having incestuous relations with his own daughter, the duchesse du Berri. Voltaire was sent to Sully, where he stayed with the duke of Sully on a magnificent estate on the Loire River. Though his surroundings were again beautiful, he longed to be back in Paris, where he had yet to make a name for himself. After a few months he appealed to the regent to lift the ban on his return, and by the fall of 1716 he was back in Paris.

FIRST TASTE OF SUCCESS

In less than a year scandal struck again, and he was accused of writing "J'ai vu" ("I have seen"), a poem defaming the regent. Though he definitely did not write the satiric piece, he could have, and in May 1717 he was arrested and jailed in the Bastille, where he spent almost a year in relatively comfortable quarters. There he worked on his writing, and eventually the real author of "J'ai vu" confessed to having written it.

When Voltaire was released in April 1718, he had finished his tragedy *Oedipus,* modeled on Sophocles' tale of the ill-fated Greek king, and the first draft of an epic poem about Henry IV.

He also adopted a new name when he left the Bastille: it was then that he called himself Arouet de Voltaire, a name soon abbreviated to Voltaire. The exact origins of the name are unknown, though critics have suggested several possible explanations for the choice; one possible explanation is that "Voltaire" is a shortened form of "*le petit volontaire*" (the little volunteer), a pet name that he was called as a child.

In November 1718, *Oedipus* opened in Paris to instant acclaim. Though the appeal of the play has not withstood the test of time, Voltaire was immediately the darling of Paris; he was famous overnight and soon wealthy, and the play broke all performance records of the era. Voltaire himself even took on a role in the play, acting poorly and risking the ruin of his own work for the sake of having a bit of fun with his audience and himself.

Soon he was asked to leave Paris again. Another anonymous satire of the regent, "The Philippics," appeared, and in May 1719 the authorities asked Voltaire to spend the summer out of the city. He spent most of the summer at Sully, where he worked on his new play, *Artemire,* another Greek-style tragedy based on Artemis, the Greek goddess of chastity and hunting. When this second play failed upon its opening in February 1720, Voltaire took the disappointment in stride and turned his attention to finishing his epic poem about Henry IV. Originally titled *The League* and later retitled *The Henriade,* the poem was published at Rouen in 1723. Voltaire had to publish the work outside of Paris because Parisian authorities were not likely to grant a permit for publication of a poem about a king who had practiced and set down policies concerning religious tolerance, especially since a later king had reversed those laws. Copies were smuggled into Paris, however, where they proved extremely popular.

In the fall of 1725 Voltaire was assaulted by thugs hired by the chevalier de Rohan-Chabot, with whom Voltaire had had a violent and somewhat petty quarrel concerning the lineage of their names and Voltaire's lack of nobility. Voltaire was outraged by the attack, but more so by the fact that no friends came to his defense or even sympathized with him. In response, he learned to fence and challenged the chevalier to a duel, but before it could take place Voltaire was arrested and thrown once more into the Bastille in April 1726. He soon offered officials a deal: if they would release him, he would leave France. The offer was accepted; in May, he was released from prison, and he soon sailed for England.

According to several biographers, Voltaire very soon secretly returned to Paris intent on finding Rohan and avenging Rohan's insults. He was unsuccessful, however, and after two months he returned to England. Very soon after his second arrival on British shores, Voltaire's sister died, adding to his despondency.

ENGLAND

In England, Voltaire found political freedom he had never experienced in his homeland. The English parliamentary system allowed for freedom of thought and action, while the French monarchy worked to suppress opposition, censoring publications and actions and imprisoning dissidents, as Voltaire himself had found out. He quickly set about to learn the English language, and soon became fluent. As an established poet and playwright, he found himself accepted in the highest social circles in London. He began to study the works of English philosophers such as John Locke, and he met and spoke with others such as Samuel Clarke and George Berkeley. He also began to study English literature, meeting authors such as Jonathan Swift and Alexander Pope.

His time in England was extremely productive, and he even published essays written in English. Voltaire found, though, that political freedom did not compensate for the lack of the elegant, cultured populace he had known in Paris. He still felt the draw of home, and he returned to Paris in 1729 after two and a half years across the Channel.

The next five years were extremely successful for Voltaire, but also typically conflict ridden. His play *Zaire,* a tragedy about a heroine who is caught up in the conflicts between religious faiths in Jerusalem, was very successful, and his *History of Charles XII* was also well received. Other publications, though, especially the *Epistle to Urania* and *Temple of Taste,* drew criticism and outrage. With the publication of his *Philosophical Letters* in 1934 (also referred to as the *English Letters,* or the *Letters on the English Nation*), opposition came to a head and Voltaire was forced to flee Paris or face imprisonment. The *Letters* included an essay entitled "Thoughts of Pascal" in which Voltaire expressed doubt as to the greatness and infallibility of esteemed French philosopher Blaise Pascal; such a position was almost heretical in the France of his day. Many of his enemies already considered him to be subversive, and the publication of the *Letters* bolstered their position. The book was banned from future publication and publicly burned.

INTELLECTUAL BONDS

Voltaire's Parisian publisher was imprisoned when the *Letters* was published, but Voltaire himself was in Burgundy, attending a wedding. He and his new mistress, Madame Emilie du Châtelet, agreed to flee to her estate in the town of Cirey in northern Champagne. There they would spend the next fifteen years, safe from the reach of Parisian authorities. Their relationship was by all accounts especially strong. Voltaire found in Madame Emilie an able companion as well as a romantic partner. She was well educated and extremely intelligent, and the two spent their time at Cirey reading, studying, learning, and sharing ideas. Their studies were wide ranging: the physical sciences, metaphysics, philosophy, poetry, history, languages, mathematics, and more. Voltaire claimed to an acquaintance that Emilie had all the qualities of the perfect friend, except that she was not a man.

During this time, Voltaire published numerous plays (*Alzire* and *Mohammed*, for example), historical works (such as *The Age of Louis XIV*), and poems (*The Man of the World, Discourses in Verse of Man*). He and Madame du Châtelet traveled extensively, visiting major European cultural centers and French courts. Voltaire also maintained a correspondence with Prince Frederick of Prussia, who eventually would become Frederick the Great. The Prussian statesman admired Voltaire, to whom he submitted his own writings. Voltaire anonymously published one of Frederick's works, the *Anti-Machiavelli*, a book refuting the view of the author of *The Prince*, with his own preface. Frederick saw in Voltaire a genius and a mentor, while Voltaire saw in Frederick the hope of a more humane type of monarch and a sensitive lover of the arts. Voltaire and Frederick met for three days in September 1740, after Frederick had taken the throne. After the meeting Voltaire returned to the Hague to supervise a second publication of Frederick's *Anti-Machiavelli*, changing content that had been acceptable when the work was published anonymously but not under the king's name. Two months later, though, he was back in Frederick's court in Remusberg, where he spent a month before returning to Brussels to meet Madame du Châtelet on her return from Paris.

Before he reached Brussels, Voltaire received news that Frederick had invaded Silesia. Voltaire's dream of a humane monarch who could philosophize and reject war while pursuing the arts was dashed, though he recovered his objectivity quickly, sending Frederick his congratulations for his victories.

As Voltaire's ties to Frederick became stronger, his relationship with Emilie weakened; while they still shared intellectual bonds, they each found new romantic interests. Voltaire began a long-lasting affair with his niece, whose husband had recently died. Emilie, however, was not so fortunate. She became pregnant by her new lover at forty-three and died in childbirth.

IN FREDERICK'S COURT

The change in Voltaire's personal life precipitated an even greater change—within a year he had moved to Prussia to join the court of King Frederick. Frederick's largesse was virtually limitless, and Voltaire, who always had a great interest in fame and fortune, took advantage of it. In the summer of 1750 Voltaire moved to Potsdam; his niece soon joined him there, and a new chapter in Voltaire's life began.

Voltaire was motivated in part by the possibility of contributing to what he saw as the ideal form of government—"enlightened monarchy." Frederick had already shown a great love for the arts and humanities. In Frederick, perhaps, he saw the perfect king: intelligent, sensitive, insightful, and strong. Who better to help shape the perfect king than he?

This chapter, though, was to be short and not so sweet. At first everything went well and Voltaire thoroughly enjoyed his freedom and privilege, but both he and Frederick were extremely strong-minded, critical people, and inevitable contentions arose. Often such conflicts arose over trivialities, such as Voltaire complaining about correcting the king's French, but other matters were far more serious, including an illegal financial deal on Voltaire's part. This deal ended in a vicious lawsuit that, while settled in Voltaire's favor, did much to diminish Voltaire's reputation in Frederick's eyes, for even Voltaire himself admitted that he had been in the wrong in the case. In March 1753, Voltaire was granted permission to leave Frederick's court, ending what he had referred to in a letter to his niece as his "three years' nightmare":

> My only plan is to desert honorably, to take care of my health, to see you again, and forget this three years' nightmare. . . . I am going to make, for my instruction, a little Dictionary for the use of kings. "My friend" means "my slave." "My dear friend" means "you are absolutely nothing to me." By "I will make you happy," understand "I will put up with you as long as I need you." "Dine with me tonight" means "I shall make fun of you this evening."[2]

Evelyn Hall goes so far as to say that "if without Voltaire the glory of Frederick would have been something less glorious, without Frederick the great Voltaire would have been greater still."[3]

Voltaire left Frederick's court in his niece's company and in possession of a book of poems that Frederick had written; apparently, its publication could have proved an embarrassment to the king. Fearing future blackmail or scandal Frederick had Voltaire and his niece arrested in Frankfurt, where the king's representative recovered the book.

GENEVA

Voltaire decided to settle in Switzerland, and in 1755 he moved to an estate he called "les Délices" ("Delights"), overlooking Lake Geneva in the republic of Geneva. His choice was interesting, for Geneva at the time was populated with Calvinists who strictly followed the laws of religious leader John Calvin—they rose at five in the morning in the summer and six in the winter; they permitted themselves no more than two dishes at any meal; and they forbade all sorts of entertainment such as musical instruments or the theater. Voltaire simply did not fit in, yet he made his home here for the next several years. Not surprisingly, he soon found himself at odds with the government of his new homeland, this time specifically due to an article in an encyclopedia that complained of the lack of theater in Geneva. Though Voltaire did not write the article himself, he was supposed to have collaborated on it, and his situation in Geneva became very uncomfortable. This discomfort led to his move to Ferney, an estate in France, which was to be his last home.

His time in Geneva, though, was punctuated by an event that profoundly shook Voltaire and strongly influenced him in writing *Candide*. On November 1, 1755, Lisbon, Portugal, was destroyed by an earthquake that killed fifteen thousand people in six minutes; another fifteen thousand were mortally wounded. The disaster occupied Voltaire's mind for a long time, and his correspondence over the next several months returned again and again to the earthquake. Of primary importance to him was the question of whether or not Alexander Pope (1688–1744), the famous Optimist philosopher, would have maintained that "Whatever is, is right," as he had written in his *Essay on Man.* Could Pope have viewed the calamity and still maintained that, as God's will, the event was right?

News of the earthquake seemed to act as a catalyst for Voltaire, forcing him to examine his own ideas and philosophies as well as those of the Optimists. How could anyone maintain that such a thing was right, especially when they were sitting in comfort at home many miles away from the carnage? The earthquake itself was bad enough, but knowing as he did that the Optimists would consider it to be a part of "the best of all possible worlds" was particularly disturbing. Voltaire's brief "Poem on the Disaster of Lisbon," published in 1756, dealt with the profound questions of living and being that Voltaire saw lacking in the philosophical system of Optimism. The seeds had been sown for *Candide,* and they were watered well by a letter from Jean-Jacques Rousseau, a fellow philosopher who had been asked by Genevan authorities to express disapproval over the poem. Rousseau's main argument seemed to be a shallow one: If people did not build houses seven stories high, there would not be so much damage in such a calamity.

FERNEY

Voltaire moved to his estate at Ferney with every intention of continuing to write, publish, and entertain freely. Because the chateau was situated on the border between two countries, he had a quick way out of France if pressure to leave intensified. During the following years, Ferney became a living example of a philosophy put into practice. Voltaire's ideas of cooperation among people and the value of working to avoid boredom and vice helped to transform a small community of fewer than one hundred people into a thriving small city of over twelve hundred. There was work for all, and Voltaire mandated fair practices in conducting business and governmental affairs. Voltaire was in his ideal world. As patron of the town, he lived out his own philosophies.

The estate also reflected Voltaire's lack of knowledge and ability concerning the visual arts. He became his own architect in reconstructing his chateau; the best that could be said of the plain, spacious, functional design was that it was not too ugly. Voltaire had never been much interested in the visual arts or architecture, and though he had spent a great deal of time in the architectural and artistic capitals of Europe, he had paid little attention to his surroundings. Nature itself was of low priority to him; as far as beauty was concerned, it seemed that nine-tenths of the beauty of an object to Voltaire lay in its possession. He loved gardens that were his gardens, and he loved the chateau at Ferney because it was his.

Despite his ownership of the estate, it might have appeared that Voltaire's many visitors had taken over the castle. Numerous guests at Ferney stayed for months or even years, without meeting their host despite flattering attempts. Voltaire's life there was pleasant but isolated. He usually stayed in bed until at least eleven o'clock, writing or reading or dictating to his secretaries. He would spend the rest of the day in the gardens or managing his estate. At first he would dine with his multitude of guests, but after a few years, he took to dining alone.

CANDIDE

Voltaire wrote *Candide* at Ferney in 1759. The book was a literary response to the philosophy of Gottfried Wilhelm Leibnitz (1646–1716), a German mathematician and scientist who had attempted to establish a philosophical system that reconciled a purely scientific explanation of the universe with a belief in a just God. Voltaire was upset by Leibnitz's assertion that of all possible worlds that God could have created, this must be the best, for God would have chosen the best. The English philosopher Alexander Pope's claim that "whatever is, is right," provided Voltaire with Pangloss's famous optimistic catchphrase "tout est bien" ("all is well") in *Candide*, and from there Voltaire set out to satirize what he perceived to be a dangerously naive outlook.

To Voltaire, the philosophy of Optimism was far too simple a perspective on life, irreconcilable with the presence of evil in the world. Why did people murder each other, steal from each other, deceive each other, harm each other? How could a world rife with the violent aberrations that Voltaire catalogues so well in *Candide*—wars and earthquakes and piracy and murder, to name but a few—be the best of all possible worlds? Voltaire was neither a cynic nor a pessimist, but he saw in Optimism a dangerous simplicity that could easily lead weak thinkers to complacency and acceptance of evil as a natural part of the course of things. With *Candide*, Voltaire effectively destroyed many of the basic ideas that formed the foundation of Optimism; after its publication, the philosophy was never again as credible or as popular. Part of the beauty of the work is that without directly challenging the theories of the Optimists, Voltaire exposed them as ignorant and un-realistic.

FIGHTING OTHER BATTLES

Voltaire's time at Ferney was also spent fighting for favorite social causes, especially related to religious and social injus-tice against individuals. His major battle was on behalf of Jean Calas of Toulouse, a Protestant accused of killing his son to prevent him from converting to Catholicism. While the family claimed that the son had committed suicide, the father was convicted of murder and executed in 1762. Voltaire took up the dead man's cause, trying to clear his name posthu-mously. In 1764 the decision of the court was reversed; though it was too late to save the dead man, his name was cleared of the conviction of murdering his son.

The aging Voltaire continued writing and working to make Ferney a successful village. By 1778 he was a national hero, and a statue in his honor was to be erected in Paris. His new play *Irene* was scheduled to open in the capital, and the urge to return to Paris became irresistible. He left Ferney in February and was received with adoration by Parisians as well as Amer-ican statesman and diplomat Benjamin Franklin who pre-sented his grandson to be blessed by Voltaire. In failing health, however, Voltaire was not allowed to attend the opening night of his play. On May 30, 1778, Voltaire died at age 83.

CONFLICT EVEN IN DEATH

Just as in life, Voltaire caused a great deal of conflict even in death. The clergy of Paris would not have agreed to bury him in holy ground even though he had written a confession of faith several weeks earlier, so his nephew, the Abbé Mignon, secretly had the body embalmed and smuggled out of the city—some accounts have the body propped in a sitting posi-tion, others lying on the seat like a sleeping traveler—and taken to the monastery of Scellieres in Champagne, where Voltaire's body was buried with full rites on June 2. The bishop of the diocese tried to forbid the burial on June 3, but it was too late.

But Voltaire's remains were not to rest in peace, as the leaders of the French Revolution had the body returned to Paris, accompanied by a procession of city officials, deputies, magistrates, opera singers, and many others, where Voltaire received a dignified burial befitting a national hero. Over seventy years later, it was discovered that his grave had been violated, probably under the orders of the Bourbons, who came back into power in 1814. Voltaire's life and thoughts had been full of irony and satire, and the treatment of the body following his death probably would have amused this student of human nature.

Voltaire left behind a vast catalog of works—plays, novels, essays, histories, letters, philosophical treatises—that challenge even the most devoted scholars. Save for *Candide*, the works of Voltaire have not survived the test of time. His plays are no longer produced with any regularity, his poems are seldom read, and though he paved the way for later historians, his history books are rarely opened outside of graduate schools. *Candide*, though, was a work of passion—perhaps his most inspired work. The gifted Voltaire lived according to his principles, always curious and critical, intrigued by life's paradoxes and intolerant of complacency.

NOTES

1. A. Owen Aldridge, *Voltaire and the Century of Light.* Princeton, NJ: Princeton University Press, 1975.
2. Peyton E. Richter and Ilona Ricardo, *Voltaire.* Boston: Twayne, 1980.
3. S.G. Tallentyre (Evelyn Beatrice Hall), *The Life of Voltaire.* New York: Loring and Mussey, 1903.

CHARACTERS AND PLOT

Baron Thunder-ten-tronckh. The master of the castle who kicks out Candide. He is soon killed when the Bulgarians invade.

Cacambo. Candide's valet and eventual traveling companion and friend. Cacambo's knowledge of South America and its people helps Candide in many ways during his travels there.

Candide. The main character, whose origin is unknown and irrelevant. His name shows who he is at the beginning of the story—a candid, innocent youth.

Cunégonde. Candide's true love, the object of his desire and of all his searches and journeys. She causes Candide's expulsion from her father's castle when she seduces him.

Cunégonde's brother (the Colonel). Never named, he's based partly on Frederick the Great. Candide first runs him through with a sword, then pays to have him sent away at the end of the story.

Don Fernando. His full name is a parody of the ridiculousness of titles; he takes Cunégonde from Candide when they arrive in Buenos Aires.

James, the Anabaptist. The only one who helps Candide in Holland; through him Voltaire points out the hypocrisy of many Christians, for though James has not even been baptized, he shows the greatest Christian charity.

The Old Woman. Daughter of a pope and a princess; Cunégonde's traveling companion; she saves Candide at the *auto-da-fe.*

Dr. Pangloss. The tutor at the castle; a philosopher whose character is a parody of the Optimist philosophers. His simplistic perspective of the world is eventually rejected by Candide.

Paquette. A servant who gives Pangloss venereal disease, then is kicked out of the castle herself, eventually becoming a prostitute. She meets Candide again late in the book.

PLOT SUMMARY

Candide's story begins in the castle of the baron of Thunder-ten-tronckh, where he is living with the baron, his 350-pound wife, their daughter Cunégonde, and a son who is not named. Dr. Pangloss is the children's tutor; his philosophy that all is for the best in the world has a profound influence on Candide and Cunégonde. Unfortunately, this influence has disastrous results: When Cunégonde sees Pangloss engaged in sexual intercourse with a chambermaid, her curiosity about sexuality is piqued, and she attempts to seduce Candide. Candide's pleasant existence at the castle ends when the baron catches them in the act and literally kicks Candide out of the castle.

Candide goes without supper that evening, and is famished and nearly frozen by the time he reaches the next town, Wald-Berghoff-trarbkdikdorff. He is penniless and half-dead, so he gladly accepts an invitation to dinner from a pair of strangers. But the men shackle him and take him away to a regiment of the Bulgarian army, where he is trained in warfare, beaten for every mistake, and brutally mistreated. In fact, when he tries to exert his free will and walk away from the army, he is forced to run a gauntlet of two thousand men thirty-six times. Soon the king of the Bulgarians declares war against the king of the Abares, and Candide witnesses the horrible atrocities of war firsthand. Eventually, he escapes and makes his way to Holland, penniless and starving.

Though Holland espouses Christian principles, Candide is met with animosity and threats of imprisonment for begging. A kind Anabaptist named James offers Candide his help. The very next day, Candide runs into a beggar who is ravaged by disease. He is revealed as Pangloss, who contracted venereal disease from Paquette, the chambermaid. He tells Candide how the castle was stormed by the Bulgarians and everyone there killed. James helps Pangloss to be cured and even hires him as his bookkeeper. Soon James has to sail to Lisbon on business, and he takes Candide and Pangloss with him.

While in sight of the ship's destination, a strong storm strikes the ship. James falls overboard and perishes. The ship is wrecked at sea, and Candide, Pangloss, and a sailor are the only survivors. The three make their way to shore just in time to experience an earthquake that destroys three-quarters of Lisbon, killing over thirty-thousand people. Amid the ruins, Pangloss and Candide are arrested by Inquisitionists, who decide to avert future disaster by offering up their prisoners in a sacrificial *auto-da-fe* ("act of faith," or execution). Three other prisoners are burned, Pangloss is hanged, and Candide is whipped. Before Candide can be tormented further, an aftershock hits the city, and he escapes to safety with the help of an old woman.

Eventually the old woman takes him to Cunégonde, who tells him how she escaped the storming of her father's castle. Candide is ecstatic to see her, but he soon learns she is a kept woman. During her wanderings, Cunégonde was captured and sold to Don Issachar in Lisbon. To ensure that he has no unpleasant entanglements with the Inquisition, Don Issachar has made a deal with the Grand Inquisitor, who had been taken by Cunégonde's beauty, to share the girl. Issachar occupies the house she is kept in and possesses her on Monday, Wednesday, and Saturday; the Inquisitor takes his place the rest of the week. To save Cunégonde, Candide ends up killing both men, and he, Cunégonde, and the old woman are forced to flee.

They reach Cadiz, Spain, where Candide is made a captain in the army by virtue of his martial skills. Soon they sail for Buenos Aires, where the army is preparing to put down a rebellion by natives. During the voyage, the old woman, who turns out to be the daughter of a pope and a princess, relates the horrible story of her life. She describes brutality after brutality, but ends by claiming that she could never kill herself, for she loves life too much.

When they arrive in Buenos Aires, Governor Don Fernando d'Ibarra, y Figueroa, y Mascarenes, y Lampourdos, y Souza immediately falls for Cunégonde and takes her as his own. Before Candide can act to free Cunégonde, the old woman hears the news that an alcalde, or official, from Spain is landing in Buenos Aires to arrest the murderer of the Grand Inquisitor. She warns Candide, who immediately flees with his valet, Cacambo. They go to Paraguay and stay with some Jesuit priests. There Candide meets his reverence, the Colonel, Cunégonde's brother. They are happy and astonished to see each other until Candide tells the Colonel that he plans to return to Buenos Aires and marry Cunégonde. At this point, the priest is insulted and strikes Candide. Regrettably, Candide strikes back and stabs the Colonel, and once more he and Cacambo are forced to flee.

Soon the fugitives are captured by fifty Oreillons, the natives of the country, who mistake Candide for a Jesuit priest. The Oreillons see the Jesuits as invaders and take revenge by cooking and eating those they catch. But Cacambo convinces the Oreillons that Candide is not a Jesuit, and the pair is set free. They wander for well over a month, running out of provisions along the way. Desperate and hungry, they stop at the bank of a river and decide to leave their fates to providence by canoeing down the river in hopes of reaching an inhabited spot. Yet, as with all Candide's adventures, the trip turns into an ordeal that concludes with a twenty-four-hour ride through a dark tunnel. At the end of the journey, however, they arrive in Eldorado.

At Eldorado the travelers find a utopian society that is quite unlike the Europe that Candide left behind. Money and jewels are so abundant that they are of little value to the inhabitants. The people are civil to each other, and everyone values work, community, and education. There is no religious conflict, and even the king greets people on his own level, embracing his guests and kissing them on the cheek. However, although Candide admires the values of the community, he soon tires of life without any struggle or conflict, and he longs to be back with Cunégonde. He arranges to leave Eldorado with many sheep laden with gifts of gold and jewels, planning to return to Buenos Aires to buy Cunégonde's freedom from the governor.

Within one hundred days of traveling, Candide and Cacambo lose all the sheep, with their loads of gifts, save two––though the riches that these carry are still enough to make both men wealthy. When they reach Surinam they meet a negro who has lost a hand and a leg; he explains to Candide that as a worker at a sugar plantation, his owners were responsible for both injuries, the former when one of his fingers was caught in a mill, the latter as punishment when he attempted to run away—such was the price that the natives paid so that people in Europe could have sugar. Thus far, Candide has clung to Pangloss's optimistic philosophy that all is well in the world, but on hearing the slave's tale, Candide rejects Pangloss's rosy and naive outlook on life, explaining to Cacambo that optimism is "the madness of maintaining that everything is right when it is wrong."

Also while in Surinam they learn that in Buenos Aires, Cunégonde has become the governor's favorite mistress, and that Candide—a known suitor—will surely be killed if he goes after her. Candide decides not to risk his life, so he gives Cacambo a great number of diamonds and arranges for him to go to Buenos Aires to buy Cunégonde from the governor. Candide instructs Cacambo to bring Cunégonde to Venice, when the deal is finished, as Candide plans to sail for Europe immediately. When Cacambo leaves, Candide is robbed of his remaining sheep and left with just a few diamonds. He buys passage on a ship headed for Europe and hires an old scholar named Martin to travel with him, paying his passage and a salary. Martin by philosophy is a Manichean who maintains that there are two principles—good and evil— which govern the world with equal power. To counter this rather cynical outlook on life, Candide clings to some of his fading optimism and points out the good side of all they experience. Martin, unconvinced, steadfastly focuses on the negative.

Martin and Candide arrive in Bordeaux, France, then take a slight detour by land to Paris, where Candide falls ill. He soon recovers and is taken to a play by an abbé of Perigord, a sleazy character who also takes him to see the marquise de Parolignac, a woman no better than he. The marquise immediately gives Candide a seat at a card table where Candide loses a great deal of his remaining money.

The next day Candide receives a letter, supposedly from Cunégonde, that tells him that she is in Paris and has been very ill. Candide and Martin hurry to see her, but he is deceived by someone who pretends to be Cunégonde in a darkened room. The deception has been set up by the abbé, and Candide is arrested after giving the fake Cunégonde a handful of diamonds. Though Candide's funds are seriously depleted Martin advises him to bribe the arresting officer. Candide takes the advice and soon leaves Paris.

Candide and Martin travel through Normandy and upon reaching the French coast, they board a Dutch ship heading for Venice. As the ship stops along the English coast on its way to the Atlantic, Candide and Martin witness the execution of a naval admiral who was accused of not having been close enough to the enemy during a battle. Candide is horrified at the spectacle, and pays the captain of the ship to avoid any future stops and sail straight for Venice.

In Venice, Candide searches for Cacambo and Cunégonde to no avail. In the meantime he runs across Paquette, arm in arm with a friar, and she tells him the story of what happened to her after she was thrown out of baron of Thunder-tentronckh's castle. She has been mistress to a long succession of men who have used her, and she is now working as a prostitute. The friar who had paid Paquette for her services also complains of a miserable life, having been forced into a monastic life by his parents. Candide is depressed by the stories, but he still wants to believe that some good exists in the world. Martin tries to convince Candide that he will not find happy people in the world. Determined to prove Martin wrong, Candide goes to see Senator Pococurante, whom people say "has never felt any uneasiness." Candide soon finds out that Pococurante is a cynic, unable and unwilling to find satisfaction in anything, and highly critical of everything. Candide has failed to counter Martin's conviction.

As Martin and Candide continue their search for Cunégonde, they stop at an inn for dinner. There, as luck would have it, they run into Cacambo. Cacambo informs Candide that Cunégonde is in Constantinople and that he had been robbed of the jewels that Candide had given him. With no finances, Cacambo was made a slave by one of the guests at the inn. This guest and five others join Candide and Martin for dinner. During the meal, the six men reveal that they are former kings who have fallen from power. They relate their sad tales and Candide gives a diamond to the king who he believes is worst off.

Cacambo arranges for passage for Candide and Martin on his master's ship, which is going to Constantinople. He tells Candide what happened to him and Cunégonde since they parted ways: After he bought back Cunégonde, their ship had been set upon by pirates, and everyone on board had been robbed and sold into slavery. Cunégonde was now a slave to a family in Turkey and had grown ugly in servitude. When the ship reaches the Bosporus Strait, Candide buys Cacambo's freedom. Candide hires a galley to take the trio the rest of the way. On board the galley Candide finds that both Pangloss and Cunégonde's brother are still alive and serving as slaves, working at the oars of the galley. Candide immediately buys their freedom, and as the group sets out to find Cunégonde, Pangloss and the Colonel tell their tales of woe that lead to their slavery.

When the group finds Cunégonde in Turkey, Candide is dismayed. She has become ugly without knowing it, since no one has told her so. Though he does not truly wish to marry her, Candide is determined to fulfill his promise of marriage because of the impertinence of her brother, who insists that

Candide cannot marry her. After consulting with his friends, Candide pays to have the baron sent away, and he marries Cunégonde. The little group settles down on a small plot of land, all working together according to their talents. Martin says, "Let us work without disputing; it is the only way to render life tolerable," and they all do so.

CHAPTER 1

Attacking *L'Optimisme*

Searching for Optimism in a Cruel World

Roger Pearson

In *Candide*, Voltaire criticizes the philosophy of Optimism. The term is generally capitalized by critics when referring to the philosophical system of English poet and philosopher Alexander Pope and German mathematician and scientist Gottfried Wilhelm Leibniz (also spelled Leibnitz by some to reflect German pronunciation). Pope's work is often characterized by the phrase "Whatever is, is right," while Leibniz maintained that this is the best of all possible worlds, for God created it. Roger Pearson, a fellow and lecturer in French at the Queen's College in Oxford, argues that just because Voltaire discredits the philosophy of Optimism as simplistic, he does not necessarily reject its ideas and theories.

Candide is said to be a satire on Optimism, but this is only partly true. It would be more accurate to say that it is a satire on systems. The philosophy of Optimism, nevertheless, is one such system, and it is the one most savagely attacked in *Candide*. . . .

In *Candide* Voltaire evidently satirizes Leibniz's Optimism not only by the illogical travesty of it which Pangloss parrots throughout the story, but also by juxtaposing it with the various atrocities and disasters of which the story provides such a seemingly inexhaustible catalogue. Rape, pillage, murder, massacre, butchery, religious intolerance and abuse, torture, hanging, storm, shipwreck, earthquake, disease, prostitution: all is well. Yet it is not just the particulars of Leibniz's system which Voltaire objects to, but even more so the belief, which he felt to be characteristic of the rationalism of

Excerpted from Roger Pearson, "Introduction," in *Candide and Other Stories*, by Voltaire. Translation, notes, and editorial material © 1990 Roger Pearson, (Oxford World's Classics). Reprinted with permission from Oxford University Press.

his age, that logic and reason can somehow explain away the chaotic wretchedness of existence by grandly and metaphysically ignoring the facts. (Hence the name 'Pangloss'.) After all, even Martin, whose views seem so much more persuasive than Pangloss's, is said by the narrator to have 'detestable principles'. They are detestable not because they are Manichean,[1] but because they are principles. Martin, no less than Pangloss, has a system, and he makes the facts fit the system rather than keep an open, 'candid' mind. Thus he predicts that the faithful Cacambo will betray Candide; which in the event he does not. . . .

This human desire to impose order on experience . . . is the mainspring of the story. Where Voltaire had previously availed himself of the Oriental tale and its associations with Eastern fatalism and the philosophy of Zoroaster, here he exploits the traditions of chivalric romance. The hero, in pursuit of his beloved (both Cunégonde and, by extension, happiness), undergoes a series of ordeals by which he proves himself worthy of her. Part of the comedy in *Candide* lies, of course, in the exaggerated and incongruous nature of these accumulated ordeals and of the quest itself. This time there is no question of the Providentialist view being taken seriously. At the end of *Candide* both Pangloss's description of the foregoing chain of events and his definition of happiness as eating candied citron and pistachio nuts are plainly absurd. Indeed they are mere words: 'That is well put,' says Candide, but what he wants is practical action, gardening. (In fact it is almost as if Voltaire himself were saying here: 'well, now you've read my fine words, stop reading and get on with it.')

But the fact that Pangloss's conclusion is ridiculed does not mean that the world of *Candide* is without order. . . . In *Candide* there is indeed order, and it is the order of education. As far as Candide himself is concerned, things happen to him suddenly and surprisingly, without rhyme or reason; and yet all the time he is turning his experiences to account. Gradually he perceives and comes to terms with the disparity between Pangloss's system and the facts of life; not only of his own life, but also of the lives of Cunégonde (Chapter 8) and the old woman (Chapters 11 and 12). By Chapter 13 he is questioning Pangloss's philosophy explicitly, and on

---

1. Manicheanism—system of philosophy of Mani (ca. 216–ca. 276), a Persian; he held that the universe is controlled by both good and evil.

reaching Eldorado in Chapter 18 he is in no doubt that Pangloss was wrong, at least about the optimal virtues of Thunder-ten-tronckh. He finally renounces Panglossian Optimism in Chapter 19 when he sees the effects of slavery in Surinam, and when he hears the applicants for the job as his companion.

THE POWER OF LEARNING

Thereafter Candide tries to think and act for himself. At the end of Chapter 20 he begins to perceive that truth may be unattainable in the abstract, and that more comfort may be derived from the human intercourse of inconclusive conversation. For all his new independence of mind, however, Candide is not yet a sure judge, and he is constantly deceived by appearance, be it the attempted fraud of the abbé from Périgord, or the seeming happiness of Paquette and Giroflée, or the contentment of Pococurante. The temptation to adopt Martin's Manicheanism in place of Panglossian Optimism is great, until in Chapter 26 Cacambo undermines it by proving faithful. After this, Candide's rejection of systems is bolstered by the renewed evidence of the sterility of intransigence: first, in Chapter 28, the comic refusal of Pangloss to change his mind ('I am a philosopher after all'), and second, in Chapter 29, the rather less comic persistence of the Baron in refusing to allow his sister to marry the unsuitable bastard Candide. In the concluding chapter he learns: (a) from the old woman, that simply opting out may be no answer, since boredom may be the greatest evil of all; (b) from the dervish, that it is best to bracket the metaphysical problem of evil; and (c) from the kindly old man, that work offers the possibility, if not of happiness, at least of a tolerable *modus vivendi.* Martin speaks for all of them when he suggests they 'get down to work and stop all this philosophizing', but even this is an abstraction, a sweeping statement. Candide's manner of expression is less dogmatically exclusive, more practical, more environmentally sound: 'we must cultivate our garden'.

It is education, then, the process of enlightenment, which gives shape to experience, and not only for Candide. Cunégonde learns that there are finer castles than that of Thunder-ten-tronckh, and the old woman learns from being digitally explored by pirates that travel broadens the mind. . . . Indeed her mind has been so broadened, and she has learnt so frequently not to trust to appearances, that she seems almost unwilling to blame the monk for robbing them in the inn at Badajoz when he is most blatantly the culprit. Worrying whether you have a leg to stand on (or a buttock to sit on) breeds futile, incapacitating caution.

At the end of *Candide,* therefore, retrospect should suggest not the absurd chain of events described by Pangloss but the Lockean[2] 'steps by which [Candide's] mind attains several truths'. By the same token, the hilarious spoof of chivalric romance conceals a symbolic narrative order of a more serious kind: the journey from one Garden of Eden to another via Eldorado, or from falsity to reality via the ideal. The castle of Thunder-ten-tronckh, supposed microcosm of the best of all possible worlds, is, of course, a fool's paradise. It is characterized by pretension—be it aesthetic (specifically, architectural), genealogical, intellectual, or even horticultural ('the little wood they referred to as their "parkland"')—and the Fall occurs as Cunégonde witnesses Pangloss giving Paquette 'a lesson in applied physiology' (during which, one later infers, he contracts syphilis). Armed with the apple of her new sexual knowledge, this Westphalian Eve seduces her Adam.

THE FINAL DESTINATION

The farm outside Constantinople is a pragmatist's paradise: not some abstract garden of 'good works' as Pangloss theologically and uselessly suggests; nor a garden like Pococurante's which you simply install at vast expense and then want to replace; but a garden of human beings in which the talent of each is a plant to be nurtured so that society as a whole benefits while the individual finds fulfilment. In this paradise male chauvinism still prevails, as the women make pastry, sew, and do the laundry, but Teutonic snobbery and Jesuit arrogance are sent back to the galleys, while Pangloss, forever imprisoned within his own risible metaphysical system, is retained. His talent, for academic debate, will at least give them something to laugh at: every paradise needs a fool. Candide's talent, of course, turns out to be that of moral leadership.

This journey from falsity to reality leads, at the centre of *Candide,* via the authentic Garden of Eden of Eldorado. Here

2. "Lockean" refers to the philosophy of John Locke (1632–1704), an English philosopher who rejected innate knowledge; he claimed that all knowledge is a result of experience.

there is true merit—aesthetic, social, intellectual, and even agricultural ('the land had been cultivated as much to give pleasure as to serve a need'). Deism is the only religion; there is a liberal monarchy; commerce is encouraged by the funding of free restaurants for tradesmen and waggoners; intellectual freedom is permitted; the spirit of scientific enquiry is fostered; the arts are encouraged; public buildings are praised (even, one assumes, by the royal family); women can join the Guards; . . . and the King's wit survives being translated. Eldorados, it would seem, do not date.

Nor does human nature change. Sex and vanity are the instruments of the Fall as Candide and Cacambo leave Eldorado in pursuit of their sweethearts and in order to show off their riches and surpass the wealth of all the world's monarchs put together. Experience will tell that neither ambition was worth the sacrifice: Cunégonde has become ugly and shrewish, and kings are either deposed and turned into carnivalesque lookalikes, or else they meet a bad end in the manner of those whom Pangloss so eruditely lists. It would have been better not to leave, and this is the lesson they should have learnt in Eldorado. Travel may broaden the mind, but wanderlust may blow it. The Incas who once lived there left to 'go and conquer another part of the world', rather as Candide and Cacambo want to go off and lord it. But, says the King, 'when one is reasonably content in a place, one ought to stay there'. And this is the right way to think of the matter, not negatively like Martin who 'was firmly persuaded that one is just as badly off wherever one is'. . . .

Candide, or Optimism, comes to no clear-cut conclusion about optimism. About Optimism, yes: as a philosophical system, Optimism is discredited, not so much (and certainly not only) because its tenets are shown to be implausible in the light of the evidence, but essentially because it is a system. As such it is as inhuman and as dangerous as all the other systems which are ruthlessly satirized in the story: the military system, the Church system, the colonial system, the caste system, and indeed the system of logic itself.

ROOM FOR HOPE

And yet the picture is not unrelievedly bleak, and there may be some grounds for optimism. First, human beings may be admirable for their will to survive, their refusal to commit physical, and what [French author] Albert Camus later called 'philosophical', suicide. As the old woman says: 'A hundred times I wanted to kill myself, but still I loved life. This ridiculous weakness for living is perhaps one of our most fatal tendencies. For can anything be sillier than to insist on carrying a burden one would continually much rather throw to the ground? Sillier than to feel disgust at one's own existence and yet cling to it? Sillier, in short, than to clasp to our bosom the serpent that devours us until it has gnawed away our heart?'

Secondly, human beings may be admirable for this very awareness of their ridiculousness, indeed for their capacity to laugh at adversity. Perhaps, even, there is some value in adversity. After all, Pococurante is the man who has everything and, precisely, is bored. He seeks to improve his garden by having a bigger and better one, but without personal effort. He never travels: people visit him (and without difficulty, unlike Eldorado). Perhaps some measure of deprivation, some evil, actually is beneficial, because it lends purpose and contrast to life. Perhaps Pope and Leibniz are not entirely wrong. And purpose would lie in developing one's own individual talents, apparently self-centredly, but ultimately to the benefit of society. (Presumably Cunégonde does not scoff all her pastries herself.)

But in the end there is only the semblance of a solution to the problem of evil in *Candide*. The dervish's view simply minimizes it but does not remove it; and the kindly old man's advocacy of work leaves much out of account. Work may prevent boredom, vice, and need, but what about intellectual and emotional fulfilment? Martin says we should stop philosophizing, but an enquiring mind is one of the more desirable human attributes. And what is happiness? Merely the avoidance of things? And what of love?

To the random chaos of existence *Candide* brings not the order of Jesrad's Leibnizian Providentialism but the literary order of a symbolic journey from a false, Germanic Eden to a state of rather muted Turkish delight. But the story offers only an illusion of closure: the final, famous aphorism fails to hide much uncertainty. . . . *Candide* is ostensibly translated from the German of one Doctor Ralph, but consists also of the addenda found in his pocket when he died at the battle of Minden. Were all the addenda found? Perhaps the final page was lost. Where reason fails, the fable provides—if nothing else, an excuse for the absence of an answer.

Using Characters to Disprove Optimism

Haydn Mason

In this article, Haydn Mason argues that with *Candide*, Voltaire is protesting the nonsensical claim of the Optimists that this is the best of all possible worlds. Mason, a professor of European Studies at the University of East Anglia in Norwich, U.K., maintains that Voltaire's characters and their tribulations are proof enough to discredit the claim, while at the same time showing that this world is not all that bad. According to Mason, Voltaire seems to be saying that with the right attitude, one can expect many good things from the world.

Voltaire had already given a foretaste of the astringent tone which was to come in *Candide* when he had written the *Histoire des voyages de Scarmentado*, probably in 1753–4. But *Scarmentado* is only an abbreviated blueprint, lacking the authorial control of *Candide*. As all the world knows, *Candide ou l'Optimisme* (to give the *conte* its full title) is a satire on Optimism, in which the philosophy of [Alexander] Pope's *Essay on Man* and [Gottfried] Leibniz's *Theodicy* received their quietus at last. The complex details of this philosophic filiation need not be examined in order to understand why Optimism was so hateful to Voltaire. Its basic defect is summed up by Candide at a moment when he can no longer overlook the horrors of this world. Optimism, he explains in answer to Cacambo's question, is "the mania for asserting that all is well when one is not." In its unrealistic cheerfulness, it is not merely an absurd philosophic viewpoint but a cruel one to boot, as Voltaire had made clear in a letter some years before. It is awful because it invites man to acquiesce in the existing situation, to say Yes to the universe . . . to give up hope and practical effort. The point is demonstrated by

Pangloss, preventing Candide from any attempt to rescue Jacques with his thesis that "Lisbon harbour had been formed expressly for this Anabaptist to drown in it." Pangloss, in his useless passivity, waits for events to happen in order to prove them right. In the best of all possible worlds, there would be no point to a *Candide*, nor indeed to any literary work except perhaps hymns of pure praise and exultation.

The *conte* is in the first place a protest against any such nonsense. Its world is full of abominations, in which man's misfortunes are exceeded only by the absurd figure he cuts; dignity is as rare as happiness in *Candide*. One critic speaks of Voltaire's satanism, of his delighting in the horrible when at work on this canvas. Of this there can be little doubt. But to see the tale as purely a savage attack would be to limit its resonance most seriously. [Voltaire scholar] J.G. Weightman has seized upon the special tone of Candide precisely when he writes:

> In this one book, the horror of evil and an instinctive zest for life are almost equally matched and it is the contrast between them . . . which produces the unique tragi-comic vibration. . . . an unappeasable sense of the mystery and horror of life is accompanied, at every step, by an instinctive animal resilience. . . . *Candide* throbs from end to end with a paradoxical quality which might be described as a despairing hope or a relentless charity.

This quality is explicitly stated by La Vieille [the old woman], when she has concluded her personal recital of atrocities suffered. From this tale of horror, perfidy and humiliation one gains a vivid impression of nonsensicality. The Moors break off their hideous massacres only to observe the five times of prayer ordained by Moslem ritual each day. The janissaries swear never to surrender to the besieging enemy and in order to keep their pledge begin to dine off their captive women when stocks run low. La Vieille, like the others, has lost one buttock when the attackers carry the fort and kill all the male defenders. This nightmarish ridiculousness is in keeping with the basic perception which La Vieille has made of human existence: however many miseries and humiliations we incur, we never give up clinging to life:

> I wanted a hundred times to kill myself, but I still loved life. This ridiculous weakness is perhaps one of our most lamentable inclinations: for is there anything more foolish than to

want to carry around continually a burden that one is forever
wanting to cast down? To hate one's being, and to cling to
one's being? In brief, to caress the serpent that devours us,
until he has eaten our heart?

It is by rational standards a folly indeed, though whether it
renders the human condition more tragic or more comic is
hard to tell. . . .

The tone is consistent with these remarks. It has often
been pointed out that *Candide* is a story where the characters do not die, or if they do are resurrected. Though generally true, this statement must be treated with caution. Apart
from the death of Jacques (the exception which proves the
rule), a few minor characters do disappear for good: the first
one referred to in the *conte*, the Baron of Thunder-ten-
tronckh, and his wife, who both perish horribly, as too does
La Vieille's mother; the wicked Vanderdendur is drowned at
sea, and all the major characters witness scenes of carnage
and destruction. In brief, the people on the forefront of the
stage all have ample experience of death; but death is, as [ex-
istentialist philosopher and author Jean-Paul] Sartre once
put it, something that happens to others. At times the leading characters come perilously close, and Candide even requests at the very beginning of his career that he be put out
of his misery when he can run the gauntlet of the regiment
no more; but once we have seen the improbable way he is
saved from this fate we can guess what will be his destiny
and the destiny of his friends: to survive.

HOPE IN THE FACE OF ADVERSITY

Cunégonde impresses this point upon him when they meet
in Lisbon. She has indeed been raped, her stomach ripped
open, "but one does not always die from these two acci-
dents." Suicide is so eccentric a practice as to be of little relevance to mankind as a whole; in all her odyssey of tribulations La Vieille has known only a dozen people who took
that way out. Hope springs eternal; although Candide comes
to realize, especially after seeing Eldorado, that Pangloss
cannot possibly be right, he still has Cunégonde to seek for,
and that is enough to sustain life. His *naïveté* is fatuous too:
"When he thought of what remained in his pockets, and
when he spoke of Cunégonde, *especially at the end of the
meal,* he inclined towards Pangloss' system." On such a fragile material basis as a good dinner theories like Optimism

are constructed and upheld. But Candide is not merely a figure of fun. He is in his foolish hopes Everyman. By contrast
'Martin n'avait rien à espérer'; and Martin turns out to be a
cardboard figure, a walking version of philosophical pessimism, much more devoid of human sensibilities than Pangloss. Martin never acts save to opine, and his opinions,
though often right because there is so much misery and
malice in the world, are also on occasion wrong; for Martin
is as morally blinkered as Pangloss: "However, some good
does exist," replied Candide. "That is possible," said Martin;
"but I am not aware of it."

This unawareness of good is as disabling as unawareness
of evil. Martin is cynical about friendship and loyalty, wrong

POPE'S "ESSAY ON MAN"

*Alexander Pope's major work is one of the strongest influ-
ences of* Candide. *In it Pope claims that all is right, for
God has so ordained it. Voltaire's* Candide *is an attack on such
optimism.*

What was the view expressed by Pope in the *Essay on Man?*
The reader who will give a little time to the four brief epistles
of this poem followed by the *Universal Prayer* so frequently
circulated with it will understand better the subject under
discussion. A few quotations from the *Essay on Man* will help
to make clear the author's thought.

Pope starts with the premise that this world must be a
planned world and that God must have chosen the best plan
for all nature and life.

> *Of Systems possible, if 'tis confest,*
> *That Wisdom infinite must form the best,*
> *Where all must full or not coherent be,*
> *And all that rises, rise in due degree;*
> *Then, in the scale of reas'ning life, 'tis plain,*
> *There must be, somewhere, such a rank as Man:*
> •   •   •   •
> *Respecting Man, whatever wrong we call,*
> *May, must be right, as relative to all.*
> •   •   •   •
> *Then say not Man's imperfect, Heaven in fault;*
> *Say rather, Man's as perfect as he ought:*
> •   •   •   •
> *Who finds not Providence all good and wise,*
> *Alike in what it gives, and what it denies?*

Emphasizing the continuity of all creation, Pope says:

in thinking that Cacambo, once possessed of riches, would never return to his master Candide. He fails to perceive that, however miserable, one human being can find consolation in the company of another; indeed, he does not seem to notice that this sense of consolation comes over him too . . . on the journey across the Atlantic with Candide. Martin is an excellent person for pointing out how little there is of virtue and happiness in the world, but he overlooks the fact that there is some. He serves a useful function as Candide's philosophical mentor in the second half of the story, Voltaire endowing him with a vivid gift for summing up a situation. When the rascally Vanderdendur, who has stolen most of Candide's wealth, is drowned at sea with all his crew, Mar-

> *Vast chain of Being! which from God began,*
> *Natures ethereal, human, angel, man,*
> *Beast, bird, fish, insect, what no eye can see,*
> *No glass can reach; from Infinite to thee,*
> *From thee to Nothing.—On superior powers*
> *Were we to press, inferior might on ours;*
> *Or in the full creation leave a void,*
> *Where, one step broken, the great scale's destroy'd:*
> *From Nature's chain whatever link you strike,*
> *Tenth, or ten thousandth, breaks the chain alike.*
>
>   •   •   •   •
>
> *All are but parts of one stupendous whole,*
> *Whose body Nature is, and God the soul;*

The last four lines in this quotation summarize excellently the idea of the universe as a *plenum* or whole and state the concept of continuity, or the chain of being, about which so much is heard in the philosophy of Optimism. The First Epistle now closes with these equally characteristic lines:

All Nature is but Art, unknown to thee;
All Chance, Direction, which thou canst not see;
All Discord, Harmony not understood;
All partial Evil, universal Good:
And, spite of Pride, in erring Reason's spite,
One truth is clear, WHATEVER IS, IS RIGHT.

Thus the universe is declared to be essentially harmonious, partial evil (or evil to the individual) contributes to the universal good, and "whatever is, is right" and is in accordance with God's fundamental plan.

Milton P. Foster, *Voltaire's "Candide" and the Critics*, Belmont, CA: Wadsworth, 1965.

tin makes a precise distinction: "God has punished this ras-
cal, the Devil has drowned the others." But Candide is not
persuaded of such a Manichean[1] arrangement, any more
than he shares Martin's belief that the world has been
formed ["to drive us wild"].

A much more likely hypothesis, and one which appears to
carry more weight with the hero, is that of divine indifference to the human lot, as outlined by the

> very famous dervish who was reputed to be the best philoso-
> pher in Turkey: 'When His Highness sends a ship to Egypt, is
> he concerned if the mice in the ship are comfortable or not?'

The best solution in the dervish's view is not to go on philosophizing as do Pangloss and Martin, but in reply to Pangloss' question to [be silent]. Martin is wrong too about the
basis of human character in equating men's rapacity with
the predatory nature of sparrowhawks, and even though
Candide's objection is feeble—"Oh!" said Candide, "there is
a great deal of difference, for freewill . . ."—he is right. There
is a difference, as the saintly Jacques, or Cacambo's loyalty,
or the old Turk in the final chapter, demonstrates. The world
contains a stupendous amount of evil but some good; the
only satisfactory picture is one which does justice to this
blend. By the end Candide has gone beyond his second
philosophical tutor Martin just as much as he has rejected
Pangloss. Despite his ingenuousness he has always been
practical-minded, wanting to rescue Jacques, turning to help
cure Pangloss of his syphilis instead of uselessly arguing
with him over the philosophical reasons for such a disease.
By nature he is equipped to 'se taire', once he is convinced
that metaphysical discussion is forever useless. At the close
of *Candide* he has become an agnostic, totally emancipated
from the teachings of his dogmatist friends.

The final resolution of the *conte*, in the garden near Constantinople, should be seen along these lines. It is not a
wholly satisfactory solution, but in the nature of things it
could hardly be, since the world of *Candide* is one of in-
tractable problems. At any time thieves could break in to
murder and destroy, or an earthquake could wreak the same
havoc as at Lisbon, even without human intervention. But it
is as suitable a spot as any, not at all a mythic place but one

1. Manicheaism—system of philosophy of Mani (c. 216–c. 276), a Persian. He held that
the universe is controlled by both good and evil.

where a viable community could be realistically envisaged in the mid-eighteenth century. A fugitive from the Old World whose hopes are as quickly dashed in the New, Candide returns a wealthy man to try the European experience afresh; but he is to discover that life for the rich and powerful is as miserable as for the poor. The final stay is to be made in a place where a limited form of civilization can exist in a small community, as the old Turk has shown; as for Parisian theatre or Venetian society, these possible delights fade into insubstantiality. . . .

THE PROBLEM OF BOREDOM

The aim of the characters in this book has been to survive; such will still be the situation at the end, though now they face a further problem arising from their new-found calm and prosperity, the problem of boredom. It is a skilful stroke of Voltaire's imagination to show this little community as thoroughly discontented in the garden at first. They seem to have learnt nothing. Cacambo is overworked and curses his fate; the three 'philosophers' seem by contrast to have endless time on their hands for disputations over metaphysics and morality; while Cunégonde and the old woman are thoroughly out of sorts. Only their discussions, useless though they are, punctuate the ennui, which is so great that the old woman wonders whether after all the atrocities of the past were not preferable. Martin draws the appropriate conclusion from their mode of existence: "man had been born to live in the convulsions of anxiety or the lethargy of boredom." The only mistake he makes is his usual one: he generalizes too readily.

Candide alone of the group has some doubts about this viewpoint, but he too has no positive ideas about how to alter the situation. They have come to the best place in the accessible world and they do not recognize its qualities; they have not heeded the king of Eldorado's advice that "when a man is tolerably well off somewhere, he should stay there."

Everything depends in the last resort on the right attitude. It will require the brusque philosophic advice of the dervish, followed by the practical demonstration given by the old Turk as to what work can achieve, to open their eyes. Candide, Pangloss, Martin all recognize at last the benefits of work, even if Martin's reasons are cloaked in habitual gloom and Pangloss characteristically thinks he has found a new final cause of man's existence. . . . Cunégonde will still be ugly, Pangloss loquacious, Martin presumably unchanging in his views: but there is room for good harvests and even (more significantly) for moral improvement: "Brother Giroflée . . . was a very good carpenter, and even became a gentleman." Martin's total fatalism has been disproved, while Pangloss' teleological explanations of their better state are self-evidently as false as all his earlier opinions. Only Candide has achieved the difficult task of renouncing metaphysics and absolutes and settling for relative values. There is no transcendental goal whatsoever at which to aim. It is sufficient if they have created a little light for themselves in a brutish world.

Voltaire's Attack on Optimism Has a Humanitarian Goal

Virgil W. Topazio

Virgil W. Topazio argues that although Voltaire is consistently critical in *Candide*, it is not a pessimistic work. With his satire Voltaire targets Optimism, romantic love, war, and women, among many other things, but Candide never loses hope though he's surrounded by discouraging people in a discouraging world. Topazio, professor and chair of the French department at Rice University at the time this article was written, suggests that Voltaire is a humanitarian who raises the readers' level of awareness that all is not as it should be in the world.

Whether *Candide* reflects pessimism in the philosophical sense of the word, or simply despair at existing circumstances, there can be little doubt about the increasing dismay with which Voltaire viewed the human condition. The "garden" of *Candide* undoubtedly conveys a measure of optimism, but it does not entirely dispel the aura of pessimism that permeates the otherwise uninspiring, even discouraging atmosphere. And this is as it should be, given the main themes of *Candide:* the connection between human conduct and the presence of evil in the world, and the reduction to absurdity of the philosophical optimism of [Alexander] Pope, [Gottfried] Leibnitz, and their defender, [Jean-Jacques] Rousseau. The survey of the world's ills is made possible by the experiences and adventures of the hero Candide. Essentially, he is naive, sincere and well-intentioned, but he is hopelessly indoctrinated with the philosophy of his master Pangloss. After each disillusionment Candide remains filled with hope, persistently mouthing Pangloss's Leibnitzian

Excerpted from Virgil W. Topazio, *Voltaire: A Critical Study of His Major Works* (New York: Random House, Inc., 1967).

phrases, ever hopeful that the realization of his dreams is just around the proverbial corner. Ironically, when Candide reaches Eldorado, in essence "the ideal of human aspiration," he is driven out, in Lester Crocker's words, by the "dynamism of his vices." This is one aspect of Voltaire's pessimistic commentary on life. Man by his very nature must strive for goals; therefore a life of perfection would in the long run become intolerable, downright unlivable, for without objectives ambition would disappear and man would vegetate. Or . . . the burden of a virtuous life would become too heavy for imperfect man to endure. Indirectly, Voltaire is probably presenting a parody and caricature of the Garden of Eden and Original Sin.

LEAVING ELDORADO

Vanity and woman are the reasons given for Candide's departure from Eldorado. The human desire to stand out over one's fellowman spurred Candide to leave with a supply of diamonds, which were meaningless in Eldorado because of their commonness, yet were capable elsewhere of giving him status and even superiority. Cunégonde, symbolizing the eternal woman, was clearly the primary reason for his abandonment of the terrestrial paradise. It is Cunégonde whom Candide was constantly pursuing. Voltaire is in effect preaching the stupidity of chasing dream-bubbles, which always burst when clutched. He emphasizes this point by having Cunégonde turn out to be ugly and waspish. Candide, the faithful and honorable lover, keeps his promise and marries her. The explanation by some critics that the marriage displayed a reversal of Voltaire's anti-feminism seems highly implausible. Voltaire rendered Candide's resignation to the unpleasant turn of events somewhat more logical by imbuing the hero with a new-found social consciousness. Still, it was the cynical and anti-feminist Voltaire who, with a glint in his eyes, said that Cunégonde had become a passable pastry cook. Certainly he was enjoying the plight of the husband and lover eternally tied to a cantankerous and ugly woman. Nor was Cunégonde's situation more enviable; she had lost her beauty and was condemned to a loveless marriage. It would be naive to suppose that the consolation derived from the knowledge of her social contribution could compensate entirely for these losses.

The numerous trials that Candide had to undergo before

achieving the spiritual and social awakening which made possible the sensible and practical ethic embodied in the conclusion would seem to indicate the difficulty of attaining this goal. One could normally have expected Candide, newly married to his long-sought Cunégonde and united with his friends, to lead a happy and contented life. Yet this did not happen for they wasted their time in fruitless speculation, which was devoid of meaningful action. Their socially erod- ing idleness resulted in a horrible ennui, and the at best helpless Candide, who never did seem to know what course of action to pursue, became more indecisive and immobi- lized. The only member of the group engaged in construc- tive work was Cacambo, because he alone worked; however, he cursed his fate. The despair and discontent of Cacambo's "garden" obviously made Cacambo's existence unacceptable as a pattern for society.

The next step involved the Turk's "garden." On the surface all seemed idyllic. With his two sons and daughters the old Turk had created a prosperous farm, which Candide ad- mired. Their dedication to work had successfully eliminated the three common dangers for man: boredom, vice, and need. Nonetheless, Voltaire's ideal was not realized by the Turk, for he eschewed all social responsibility. As a result, there could be little hope for social improvement in a prolif- eration of similarly self-centered units. By contrast, Can- dide's "garden" represented a larger group, equally dedi- cated to useful work and likewise involved at the social level, thereby holding out hope for the future while satisfying the needs of the present. Not that the tinge of pessimism de- picted by the "shrinkage" in the Turk's life had completely vanished from Candide's "garden." Pangloss after all re- mained Pangloss; he was philosophizing to the end so much so that Martin found it necessary to silence his perpetual flow of talk with advice that closely resembled the Turks. "Let's work without reasoning; that's the only way to render our life bearable." And to a certain degree, Candide himself revealed the lingering element of despair in their lives when, in answer to the old woman's question as to which was preferable—to be subjected to all the misfortunes that had been their lot or to remain there in complete idleness— he replied: "That's a big question." The adoption of the work routine did improve the situation deplored by the old woman, yet in spite of the marked "progression from pessimistic drift to meliorism," and the promise now held out by the future human wickedness with its concomitant miseries had not been eliminated. Voltaire succeeded in pointing out what direction to take; he had likewise focused attention on the human ills to be avoided or cured. Now it remained for man to persevere on the path set by the cooperation and good will demonstrated by the members of Candide's "garden," and hopefully work toward a better tomorrow. In this respect, despite the reservations noted, "the wisdom of the Conclusion is not narrow and disappointing, but excitingly dynamic, expansive, and challenging at every level of the civilized adventure."

THE SCOPE OF THE NOVEL

The tremendous scope of *Candide* is an important contribution to the excellence of the work. It presents . . . a synthesis of Voltaire's thought. The variety of ideas is greater than in *Zadig* [his previous novel], and they are somewhat more developed. A mere catalogue, albeit incomplete, of the subjects treated in *Candide* suggests the breadth of Voltaire's ideational canvas: pride of rank; court flattery; human greed; medicine; women and romantic love; political and social injustice; corruption of courts and judges; philosophical optimism; Providence; the concept of Free Will; religious intolerance, dogmas, and fanaticism; war, music, art, and literature—in short, virtually every field of human endeavor. The examples of each are legion; a few will suffice to illustrate the Voltairean approach.

Special note should be taken of Voltaire's treatment of war, one of his favorite targets. *Zadig, Babouc,* and *Micromégas* had already leveled attacks against its stupidity and inhumanity. Voltaire particularly deplored the role played by the Church and its representatives. Never did they preach against this crime that combines the most wicked aspects of human conduct: pillage, rape, homicide, and wholesale devastation. "Instead, the good priests solemnly and ceremoniously blessed the standards of the murderers; and their confreres sang, for money, Jewish songs, when the earth was soaked with blood." In *Candide* the "Te Deums" were said in both armies, to give thanks for victory or to stave off defeat (even as they are today). All of Candide's experiences with the Bulgares, after being expelled from the baron's estate in Westphalia, and especially those of Cuné-

TURNING *CANDIDE* INTO MUSIC

This short passage from Andrew Porter explains how Leonard Bernstein tried to indicate the mood of Candide *through music. Bernstein wrote* Candide, *a work that he classified as an operetta, in 1955–56. The show opened in late 1956 to moderate success.*

Alexander Pope ended the first part of his *Essay on Man* with the chilling line "One truth is clear, Whatever is, is right." (In context, the effect is not quite so stoically bleak; the next part of the *Essay* opens with "Know then thyself, presume not God to scan,/The proper study of mankind is man.") Part II of Handel's noble musical drama *Jephtha* closes with a stern tragic chorus:

> How dark, O Lord, are thy decrees! . . .
> All our joys to sorrow turning,
> All our triumphs into mourning . . .
> Yet on this maxim still obey:
> WHATEVER IS, IS RIGHT.

It was to counter such thought that Voltaire wrote *Candide*. And in the latest score of *Candide* there is a recurrent 5/4 chorale, entitled "Universal Good," with words newly written by Bernstein and Wells. Its first statement, unaccompanied, is affirmative, "We have learned and understood,/Everything that is, is good"; there it clinches the ensemble "The Best of All Possible Worlds." The chorale returns at the start of Act II, unaccompanied, sung by the chorus, but now—after the Westphalian war, after the Lisbon earthquake, after the Inquisition—the words are questioning: "Have we learned, and understood,/Everything that is, is good?" Again chorally, but now accompanied, and in a different key, it introduces the finale, and this time the words, adapted by Bernstein from Hellman, make a different affirmation: "Life is neither good nor bad. Life is life, and all we know." This is the "moral" of the piece, and it swells into the C-major finale led by Candide:

> And let us try before we die
> To make some sense of life.
> We're neither pure nor wise nor good;
> We'll do the best we know.

In this latest edition of *Candide*, a musical idea conceived in 1954 is taken up and given "definitive" utterance.

This passage from "Candide: An Introduction," by Andrew Porter, © 1991 Andrew Porter (from *Bernstein's "Candide"* compact disc, 1991 Deutsche Grammophon).

gonde and the old woman, highlight the inhuman practices of the "heroic butchery" called war.

Some may become justifiably incensed by the glaring inconsistency between Voltaire's precept and his actions. He made money from the shipping of military supplies, and he tried to sell armored weapons, first to France, later to Catherine the Great. These actions, the full story of which remains unknown, can scarcely erase the overwhelming evidence of Voltaire's continuing hatred of war. (In this connection, it may prove worthwhile to recount an incident that demonstrates the danger of relying on incidental quotations from the author himself, or attempting to construct a philosophy and a life around stories that are not fully known and documented. A graduate student . . . one day questioned an eminent professor's interpretation of Voltaire by citing chapter and verse to prove Voltaire had said just the opposite. The professor replied with a smile that combined human understanding and Voltairean irony: "Voltaire may have said exactly what you attribute to him, but, you see, even though he said that, he did not mean it." Just as with the work of Voltaire, the lesson remained long after the smiles had vanished.)

MORE TARGETS OF SATIRE

In *Candide* the attacks on religious dogmas, superstition, intolerance, and fanaticism are somewhat commonplace. The barbarity of the Inquisition is pointedly denounced. The inquisitors, Voltaire notifies us in a matter-of-fact way, had discovered an infallible way to prevent the recurrence of earthquakes—the presentation of a beautiful auto-da-fé. Immediately after one of these entertaining spectacles, "the earth trembled anew and went into a violent upheaval." An inquisitor is also used to highlight the immorality of Churchmen; he became the rival of Issachar for Cunégonde's favors. And more piquantly and maliciously, Voltaire has the old woman reveal, during the recital of her licentious past, that she was the daughter of a pope.

At times the full force of the satire was driven home quite succinctly. For example, the pride of the Spanish was satirized by the use of a name, given without comment, Don Fernando d'Ibaraa y Figueora y Mascarenes y Lampourdos y Souza. The excessive pride of the Germans, on the other hand, is pricked by numerous references to Cunégonde's seventy-two quarters, which placed her hopelessly beyond Candide's social level. The Eldorado episode is derogatory toward court flattery at the French court and human greed in general, among other things. In his dealings with the shipowners, Candide was thoroughly fleeced; even more avaricious, however, were the publishers, against whom Voltaire carried on a personal vendetta, having suffered so often at their hands. Judges and doctors are, naturally, lampooned. When Candide fell ill in Paris, the doctors flocked to his bedside, having learned that he was rich. Martin commented "I remember having been ill in Paris during my first trip; I was very poor, therefore, I had neither friends, religious attendants, nor doctors, and I got cured." The charlatanry or simple ineptitude of doctors never escaped Voltaire's barbs, and eighteenth-century medicine offered him a wealth of material for such observations as: "However, by means of medicines and bleedings, the illness of Candide became serious." Throughout his life, Voltaire despised gambling, all the more so because Emilie had been such a devotee of it. Drawing on personal experience, Voltaire related in *Candide* that our hero was cheated out of 50,000 francs, after which they dined gaily.

Women and romantic love are recurrent targets in *Candide* of Voltaire's derision and cynicism just as they were in *Zadig* and his other works. All the women in *Candide* are pictured as selfish, cheap, heartless, and sometimes just vicious. The old woman and Paquette are the worst specimens, but Cunégonde was quite willing to abandon Candide, her devoted lover, because the Spanish grandee was richer and more powerful. To reach this momentous decision, Cunégonde required only "a quarter of an hour." At a supper in Paris, during which the conversation was typically banal, insipid, and slanderous, a young marquise noticed the two large diamonds on Candide's fingers. She "praised them so earnestly, that they passed from his fingers to those of the marquise." And there is the farcical scene in which an abbé employed a young woman to impersonate a sick Cunégonde in order to extort more diamonds from Candide. Instead of arresting the abbé or the young woman, the police seized Martin and Candide, who, fearing the uncertainties of legal procedure, preferred to bribe the officials to insure their liberty. A visit to Pococurante, a Venetian gentleman most appropriately named, offered Voltaire the opportunity to satirize the chicanery and hypocrisy in music, art, and literature. Pococurante, whom Voltaire claimed to resemble, was a cynic, bored with everything. Yet many of his judgments are still sound and valid today.

THE ATTACK ON OPTIMISM

The main attack centers on the philosophy of optimism primarily through the character Pangloss, who symbolizes vain speculation and metaphysical pretensions. Voltaire presents him as a teacher of "métaphysico-théologo-cosmolo-nigologie." The sheer futility of argument over things beyond the ken of man is demonstrated by a fruitless discussion between Candide, the faithful disciple of Pangloss, and the more realistic Martin. "They debated for a full two weeks on end, and at the end of that time, they were as advanced as on the first day." Sometimes the object of Voltaire's satire is multiple, as in the following sentence, wherein Rousseau, optimism, and the Jesuits are simultaneously subjected to ridicule: "After all, the state of pure nature must be good, since these people, instead of eating me, showed me a thousand kindnesses once they knew I was not a Jesuit." (This is Candide's exclamation, after having been spared by the Oreillon savages.) Faulty logic was on occasion deliberately used with telling effect, as in Pangloss' rebuttal to Jacques' recital of evil and misery: "'All that is indispensable,' replied the one-eyed doctor; 'individual misfortunes account for the general good; so that the more individual misfortunes there are, the better everything in general is.'" The irony behind this defense of optimism lies in the fact that Pangloss has just lost an eye and an ear as a result of the syphilis Paquette had given him. And as Pangloss sang the praises of benevolent Providence, "the air darkened, the wind blew hard from all directions, and the ship was engulfed by a horrible tempest, within sight of the port of Lisbon"—the site, significantly, of the disastrous earthquake that had actually taken over 30,000 lives and wreaked incalculable property damage. In Voltaire's earthquake, all the passengers on the ship drown except Candide, Pangloss (the tale must go on after all), and the scoundrel who had drowned the virtuous Anabaptist Jacques. The preservation of the last of these three is an insidious Voltairean stroke to underscore the type of justice practiced by Providence.

Is it any wonder, when the scope and passionate strength

of *Candide* are taken into account, that [author] Anatole France was able to refer to *Candide* and [Miguel de Cervantes'] *Don Quixote* as two "manuals of pity and indulgence, bibles of goodwill"? Such is the blindness of prejudice, however, that, in the face of this monumental evidence of Voltaire's humanitarianism, he has actually been compared by a later commentator to a vulture living by and on the ruins he created around him.

CHAPTER 2

Eldorado and the Gardens in *Candide*

READINGS ON
CANDIDE

The Symbols of the River and the Garden

Manfred Kusch

Manfred Kusch argues that the Edenic qualities of Eldorado in *Candide* are suspect. The "garden" of Eldorado, Kusch maintains, symbolizes the problem of
stagnation resulting from intellectual and geographical
isolation. The river that carries Candide and Cacambo
to Eldorado, on the other hand, represents dynamic
movement and progress, a state of being preferable to
the stasis of the isolated Eden. Kusch, an assistant professor at the University of California, Davis, has written articles on eighteenth-century French fiction.

The garden represents one of the oldest, most elementary,
and at the same time, most versatile spatial structures in art
and literature. In its basic form it constitutes a closure con-
taining a rationally controlled system surrounded by an often amorphous wilderness. Throughout history the garden
and, by implication at least, the space surrounding it, have
been invested with the most divergent significations. It appears as the locus of virtue, piety, harmony, lust, and glut-
tony, to mention but a few examples. It has served as a symbol of man's civilization and, in other cases, as an insular
refuge for nature in a threatening ocean of civilization.

But the closure of the garden is never complete. In order
to relate the inside world to the world outside, in order to
demonstrate the marked qualitative difference between garden and wilderness, man must be permitted or obliged to
pass from one to the other. In fact, the possibility of passage
is a necessary condition of the binary division of the world
into order and disorder, harmony and chaos, the garden and
the non-garden. Thus every garden has a gate (The gate is,
on the one hand, part of the closure . . . and thus underlines
the absoluteness of the world represented by the garden. But

Excerpted from Manfred Kusch, "The River and the Garden: Basic Spatial Models in
Candide and *La Nouvelle Héloïse,*" *Eighteenth-Century Studies*, Fall 1978, vol. 12, no. 3,
pp. 1–15. Copyright © 1978 American Society for Eighteenth-Century Studies. Reprinted
with permission from Johns Hopkins University Press.

it also functions as an indicator of the garden's "otherness," an acknowledgment of its location next to, or in the midst of, a different world). And in most cases the function of the gate is narrowly restricted: it serves either as entrance or as exit. Indeed the function of the gate is of such importance that we may classify gardens according to whether their gates are entrances or exits. Thus the most widely treated garden model in Western culture, the garden of paradise, exists in two distinct forms: the garden of Eden at the beginning of history, characterized by a gate functioning solely as exit, and the Celestial Paradise awaiting man beyond death and history, a garden to be entered into, but without exit.

IMAGES OF EDEN

We may assume that the garden equipped with an exit is the original model for all subsequent gardens, although it is, of course, dialectically linked to the "entrance garden." It is also the least problematical of the two. Placed in the distant past, its perfection appears plausible as it is guaranteed by God's omniscience and man's ignorance. Also, the superior quality of paradise can become visible only after man has been banned from it forever. As direct verification and logical exploration are epistemological modes linked to the structure of continuous space and time outside the garden, Eden can be safely invested with attributes which would be considered exaggerations outside it. The garden of paradise can be experienced only in ignorance, it can be known only nostalgically from the outside. The only path connected with the garden of Eden is a path leading downward and away from it.

This irreversibility of movement emanating from paradise is variously indicated in art and literature by locked doors, an angel with a flaming sword, and/or, particularly in medieval paintings, a river flowing from a spring located inside the closure of the garden. In this context, the river, more than any other symbol, represents the beginning of progressive historical time and degradation outside the stasis of paradise. Interestingly, the river often emanates from a spring represented as a tranquil and crystalline pool or basin. As water appears, so to speak, magically from the ground, the question of its origin (its history) is not raised, just as the origin of the world and of man is not explained in logical fashion, but rather as magic. As we shall see, the same freedom from logic can no longer be maintained when man and the river approach the garden from the outside, the realm of coherent progression. . . .

The notion of the "exit garden" is inseparably linked to the notion of an "entrance garden." The loss of Eden implies a desire to return to, or enter into, a garden similar to the one left behind. . . . The structure of the garden's definition (its closure and gate) and the detailed structure of its interior become the proving ground for man's views of himself and his world, and the expression of his desires and inherent contradictions. The construction of gardens becomes more than all else a philosophical and ideological activity, and it should not surprise us that the *siècle philosophique* [philosophic century] was also a century of gardens. . . . We find a great number of gardens and utopias in the major works of the leading writers.

While there are, of course, many complex reasons in each individual case for the specific preoccupation with gardens, the abundance of garden models and garden debates during the eighteenth century is, I think, the expression of a gradual but profound intellectual revolution. With the increasing challenge to—and conscious destruction of—old models and traditions, writers and thinkers become aware of the necessity of constructing new models for a new mankind and their responsibility toward them. . . . To illustrate two fundamentally different solutions to the problems raised by the coexistence of the closed garden and the continuous river, I shall analyze in this essay a garden in one of the most representative works of the eighteenth century, Voltaire's *Candide*. . . .

Although I am, of course, aware that . . . literary works and their gardens have many complex links with literary traditions, historical contexts, and the writers' personalities, I would like to limit my discussion to a purely structural and intrinsic analysis. . . . I would like to begin my analysis with a question that may at first seem rather gratuitous, but which, as I hope to show, helps to draw attention to important structural assumptions . . . in Voltaire's *Candide*. . . . What happens to the river that flows into Eldorado?

ELDORADO

As we remember, Candide and Cacambo are just about to give up during their walk across South America, when they conveniently encounter not only a river, but also an empty boat perched on its bank. They accept the obvious invitation of Providence, embark, and are soon swept along toward an uncertain destination: "Une rivière," observes Cacambo hopefully, "mène toujours à un endroit habité."[1] After a voyage whose progression is measured by varying landscapes: "des bords tantôt fleuris, tantôt arides, tantôt unis, tantôt escarpés"[2] and the increasing width of the river: "La rivière s'élargissait toujours"[3] they arrive suddenly at a towering cliff into which the river disappears while narrowing its course and accelerating its speed. Candide and Cacambo are drawn into the darkness of the underground passage and emerge, "au bout de vingt-quatre heures"[4] in a landscape that is at once perfect ("partout l'utile était agréable"[5]) and closed ("ils découvrirent un horizon immense, bordé de montagnes inaccessibles"[6]). After having been chased from the "paradis terrestre"[7] of the "château de monsieur le baron de Thunderten-tronckh"—a prime example of an "exit garden" that could be enjoyed only so long as Candide was totally ignorant and Pangloss omniscient—Candide seems to have arrived in another garden of perfection. After traveling through the wilderness of the world beyond paradise and by riding on the river of history that emerged from the garden of Eden (the progressive voyage of Candide is structurally related to the river), Candide enters a closure through a narrow, one-way gate: "Il est impossible de remonter la rivière rapide sur laquelle vous êtes arrivés par miracle"[8] observes the king of Eldorado, adding; "Les montagnes qui entourent tout mon royaume sont droites comme des murailles."[9]

While Eldorado is, in this way, cut off from the wilderness that occupies the limitless space beyond the protective ring of mountains, it is not totally disconnected from the world outside. The link of Eldorado with the historical world is found in the fact that the outsider Cacambo speaks the language of the Eldoradans, and in the account given by the *vieillard* who traces the story of his family (his father was an eyewitness to "les étonnantes révolutions du Pérou"[10]) and provides a coherent explanation for the closure of his country. Just as the swift river flows into the exitless stasis of El-

1. A river always leads to some kind of habitation. 2. now covered in flowers, now bare of vegetation, now flat, now steep 3. The river grew wider and wider. 4. twenty-four hours later 5. whatever was useful was also agreeable 6. They came to a vast open space surrounded by impassable peaks. 7. earthly paradise 8. It is impossible to return up the rapids which, by a miracle, you managed to come down. 9. The mountains which surround my kingdom are ten thousand feet high and as sheer as a city wall. 10. extraordinary upheavals in Peru

dorado, violent historical events have led to a quasi-timeless state of happiness guaranteed by historical ignorance: "Je suis fort ignorant, et je m'en trouve bien,"[11] proudly proclaims Candide's host when Cacambo wants to know the history of the country.

But while an unbroken connection with the historical past and the physical link of the flowing river with the world outside clearly add to the probability of Eldorado's existence, they also pose a serious problem for the plausibility of its continued survival outside historical progression. Since the stasis of perfection (by definition) excludes directed movement, it is hard to imagine the motivation and direction of any activity in Eldorado that would go beyond accidental survival and empty meditation. Thus it must appear puzzling that the Eldoradans send their children to school, cultivate the arts, and profess a deep interest in the mathematical and physical sciences. These activities clearly go counter to the ideological and physical structure of the country. Research has to do with the expansion of knowledge, it aims at overcoming the strictures of unsatisfactory definitions. It is hard to imagine how one can stay happily ignorant of the world at large and conduct physical and astronomical experiments at the same time. To underline the improbability of coexistence between the conflicting desires of progression and expansion on the one hand and conservation and immobility on the other, Voltaire integrated a good number of features into his design of Eldorado that function as indicators of a fiction too good to be true. Beautiful female palace guards and roast hummingbirds are only two of the more obvious ones.

THE PROBLEM OF ISOLATION

If we think of life as a voyage—Candide's travels confirm this interpretation—and if we view history as a process (teleological or not), the closure of Eldorado must appear problematical. The containment of the movement of life and history within the limits of an ideal construct will in the end bring about the cessation of all movement. Happiness then becomes synonymous with stagnation and, ultimately, with death.

Candide and Cacambo understand this principle very well. "Si nous restons ici, nous n'y serons que comme les autres,"[12] observes Candide in an effort to persuade

11. I know very little about things, and that suits me well enough. 12. If we stay on here, we'll simply be the same as everyone else.

Cacambo to continue with him on their way. As movement slows in the closure of the garden, the ups and downs of life and history are evened out, dynamic differences are replaced by static essences, and homogeneity rules supreme. As the once turbulent river is left without an exit from the closed valley of Eldorado, it is bound to become a homogeneous and level body of water, a lake, perfectly calm and without direction.

So long as the garden is fed by a stream, so long as the garden is entered from the outside, that is, so long as utopia is derived from notions valid in the outside world, it will require death as a prerequisite for the enjoyment of its perfection. Thus Candide and Cacambo climb the walls of Eldorado ostensibly in order to resume their quest for Cunégonde; but the quest, a cognitive and physical movement aiming at goals hidden behind apparent closures (closures that have to be *overcome*), is also the means by which Candide and his friend escape from certain death by drowning. For Voltaire, Man, as an historical being, can never attain the stasis of perfect happiness within the course of his life. Sooner or later the river will overflow the walls of the garden and continue on its way. It will also drown those who choose to remain.

Yet despite the unmasking and ironic devaluation of the two basic garden models, Voltaire does not reject the garden as a programmatic structure altogether. After having been chased from the paradise of perfect ignorance and after climbing out of the paradise of stagnation, Candide finally settles with his friends in a rural area of Constantinople where, we are told, they go about cultivating a garden. Critics have advanced many interpretations of what exactly Voltaire may have meant when he concluded Candide's long journey with the now proverbial observation: "Cela est bien dit, mais il faut cultiver notre jardin."[13] From a structural point of view the answer is quite simple and concrete. Seen in the context of the preceding two models, the final garden of *Candide* is distinguished by its lack of definition; it is an "open" garden. Neither an "exit" nor an "entrance" garden, it is a chosen field of productive activity. Voltaire rejects the model of the garden of Eden as a narrow-minded closure inhabited by intellectually blind people; the Celestial Paradise on earth, the utopian "entrance garden," is nothing but a dream from which the hero

13. That is well put, but we must cultivate our garden.

has to rise or in which he must drown; while the garden evoked in the story's final sentence is appropriately open to individual interpretation. The concept of the garden as a fixed structure is deemphasized in favor of the more important concept of the *process* of cultivation.

This may indeed be one of the reasons why *Candide* has emerged as one of the classics of Western literature. By pointing to the problematical relationship between the garden and the river, between being and becoming, static closure and dynamic openness, between myth and history, description and narration, *Candide* is in many ways similar to Cervantes' *Don Quixote*, the perhaps most powerful prototype of realistic fiction. Just as Don Quixote's and Sancho's dreams of an island of their own fall victim to the reality of continuous space, time, and thought, Candide's Eldorado is doomed to succumb to the river which not only comes from somewhere, but also has to continue on its way. . . .

As Voltaire had suggested in his treatment of Eldorado, the desire for perfection and permanence contains its own negation as it implies the precondition of death. His heroes therefore chose to climb out of the realm of perspectiveless immersion in order to seek their satisfaction in the pursuit of distant goals. Instead of seeking the shade of secluded refuges, they opted for the often ironic light of the Enlightenment, and the instructional benefits of *le voyage*. . . . Voltaire suggests that man cannot stay but has to travel on the river of history.

Eldorado as an "Impossible Dream"

Donna Isaacs Dalnekoff

Eldorado is an ideal society, claims Donna Isaacs Dalkenoff, but one that Voltaire satirizes as an "impossible dream." Dalnekoff explores Eldorado's financial, religious, social, and political institutions to show how Voltaire has set up the country as a foil. Eldorado exists, she claims, to point out the shortcomings of the world outside its mountain walls. Dalnekoff has published other articles in *Studies on Voltaire* and *Neophilologus*.

The meaning of the Eldorado episode in *Candide* has been the subject of extensive critical debate. Does it represent the author's ideal, his vision of the perfect society, or does it represent a false paradise, to be rejected by the perspicacious reader as it is by the protagonist? If Eldorado is the perfect society as far as Voltaire is concerned, is it portrayed as one that all or some of humanity can possibly attain or at least approach to some degree, or is it portrayed as an impossible dream, incapable of realization by man, incompatible with his nature?

The literary method employed by Voltaire in portraying Eldorado has also puzzled critics. What is the significance of the manner of description, of the inclusion of certain kinds of details and the total absence of others? Why is the society endowed with a particular atmosphere and set of features? The pursuit of such questions has elicited various justifications of and attacks upon the artistry of the episode. . . .

ASPECTS OF UTOPIA

In contrast to the first six places through which Candide has passed, Eldorado, whether a true or false ideal, is a utopia in a much narrower sense of the word, with the conventional

Excerpted from Donna Isaacs Dalnekoff, "The Meaning of Eldorado: Utopia and Satire in *Candide*," *Studies on Voltaire and the Eighteenth Century*, vol. 127. Copyright © 1974 The Estate of Theodore Besterman. Reprinted with permission from the author.

features of this literary phenomenon. Voltaire did not invent Eldorado, but read about such a country in the course of his research for the *Essai sur les mœurs* (1758). His sources told him of a place where, according to legend, a group of Incas had taken refuge after the Spaniards had conquered their empire. It was said to be a place of fabulous riches, and therefore named the golden one, Eldorado, by the Europeans, who in their avarice, made it the object of an intense, but always unsuccessful search. Eldorado is thus by tradition a country of marvels, an object of desire, and at the same time a place whose reality is unproven and dubious. . . .

It is a basic characteristic of a utopian community that it be radically cut off from the world outside. More's Utopia was deliberately cut off by Utopus who dug an artificial channel to transform a peninsula into an island. Even Rabelais's Thélème, although an abbey without walls, had an inscription on its gate designed to warn away all but the select few. It is thus that the utopia preserves its integrity which would otherwise continually be subject to corrosion. At the same time however, this cutting off casts an ambiguous light over the reality of the utopia as well as its relevance to the problems of the world outside.

[Voltaire scholar William F.] Bottiglia, in his analysis of *Candide*, asserts that Eldorado serves as an ideal, which he defines as a 'standard of perfection supremely desirable but not fully attainable, though more or less approachable'. Its function is to 'serve as a lure so powerful that it seems fully attainable', although by definition it is 'beyond complete realization'. While Bottiglia is correct that Eldorado has features that seem highly desirable, Eldorado is presented as an ideal of a curiously paradoxical kind, whose approachability, not only its attainability, is very much in question. The journey to Eldorado is described in such terms as to emphasize its inaccessibility, as is the departure from it further on. . . . That Eldorado only exists at the price of its absolute isolation, is a point made clear by the old sage who receives Candide and Cacambo in his home. The rule that no inhabitant may leave the kingdom is what has conserved Eldorado's 'innocence' and 'felicity'. The facts of its geography have sheltered it from the Europeans who would otherwise kill every last one of the inhabitants in their rapacity for gold. Eldorado does not offer itself as an inspiration to the nations of the globe, for it is a condition of its survival to remain unknown. It is a society that is exceedingly fragile and in need of careful sheltering from the reality without.

The magnificent riches of Eldorado are an important cause of its need for protective isolation. The wealth of Eldorado is described most graphically, while so many other aspects of this society are merely touched upon. In the first village where Candide and Cacambo set foot, the first sight that they see is of children playing a game of horseshoes with gold pieces, emeralds, and rubies, 'dont le moindre aurait été le plus grand ornement du trône du Mogol'.[1] These objects which Candide and Cacambo gather carefully and later offer in payment for their dinner at an inn, are merely the pebbles of the road as far as the inhabitants of Eldorado are concerned and of no intrinsic value whatsoever. Bottiglia remarks correctly that the episode of the children 'illustrates the unreality of Eldorado, parodies actual and extraordinary voyages, and satirizes by contrast human notions of wealth', but does not examine the significance of how this is accomplished. It is a characteristic of utopian literature to satirize the economic systems of real society and the lust for gold and silver that the moralist in the Christian tradition regards as one of the seven deadly sins. . . . While in the real world of Europe gold and silver are associated with what is noble and exalted, in Utopia they are associated with what is despicable and low. While Europeans enslave themselves to gold and degrade themselves for it, in Utopia gold binds the slaves and serves the basest functions. Voltaire follows in this tradition in that he employs the device of estrangement to suggest the intrinsic worthlessness of gold; the inhabitants of Eldorado refer to it as 'la fange de notre terre'.[2] It is clear here however, as throughout Voltaire's writings, that he is not one who scorns luxury. In Eldorado material riches are held in little esteem only because they are so abundant, and they are employed to enhance the enjoyment of life. The attitude of the Eldoradan children to them is identified by Candide ironically with the attitude of young European princes who have had a fine upbringing: 'Il faut que les enfants des rois de ce pays soient bien élevés puisqu'on leur apprend à mépriser l'or et les pierreries'.[3] In Europe the contempt for riches is a snobbery of those who

1. The smallest of them would have been the greatest ornament on the Mogul's throne. 2. the pebbles and dirt of our land. 3. The royal children here must be very well brought up if they're taught to turn their noses up at gold and precious stones.

possess them. Moreover, it appears that in Eldorado there is another substance that is to gold and precious stones what in the world outside gold and precious stones are to pebbles and sand. Of the portal of the king's palace, the narrator writes: 'il est impossible d'exprimer quelle en était la matiére. On voit assez quelle superiorité prodigieuse elle devait avoir sur ces cailloux et sur ce sable que nous nommons or et pierreries'.[4] It is only from our perspective that the pebbles and mud of Eldorado are valuable. The Eldoradans have their own scale of values whose bottom is our top. . . .

The fundamental satiric point that emerges with regard to the riches of Eldorado is that European man is such that he only considers wealth to be valuable in as much as it raises him above his fellow man, in that its distribution is uneven. In order to savour really the luxuries of Eldorado, Candide and Cacambo feel they must take them out into the real world. . . . They are not content till they can flaunt their wealth before others and show themselves superior. Wealth can only have meaning for them and give them true pleasure in a place where it is scarce and they are among the lucky few to possess it. There it can afford them power, put them beyond the authority of the rulers of the multitude, and buy them the women they desire. Cagily, Cacambo requests from the king only several sheep loaded with provisions and with what he now refers to as 'de cailloux, et de la boue du pays'.[5] Just a short while earlier, he had attempted to pay for his dinner at the inn with the substances he now disparages.

SATIRE OF RELIGION

The nature of the religion of Eldorado is revealed through the discussion that Candide and Cacambo hold with the old sage, rather than being demonstrated through action or event. This discussion has a typical satiric structure juxtaposing a European traveller with a member of a foreign society. The traveller, by his naive and foolish questions and assumptions, unwittingly exposes himself and his own society to satiric attack. The very fact that Candide brings up the subject of religion is placed in a ridiculous light by the narrator's parenthetical explanation that it is a result of his 'goût pour la métaphysique',[6] which in the context of the work has

4. There are no words to describe what it was made of, which in itself gives some idea of just how prodigiously superior it was to the sand and pebbles we call 'gold' and 'precious stones'. 5. pebbles and some of the local dirt 6. passion for metaphysics

connotations of absurdity. Candide's first question is whether the country has a religion, and provokes a shocked response from the old man as to how he can doubt it and whether he takes the Eldoradans for ingrates. Through this response, atheism is implicitly attacked; it is exposed as contrary to human reason and decency. As the discussion continues, the same is true of the multiplicity of religions, polytheism, prayer, and the existence of a special caste of priests. Candide ingenuously exposes the perniciousness of monks in his surprised question which makes use of the device of ironic juxtaposition: 'Quoi! Vous n'avez point de moines qui enseignent, qui disputent, qui gouvernent, qui cabalent, et qui font brûler les gens qui ne sont pas de leur avis'?[7]

The discussion of religion has been cited as evidence by those who would prove that Eldorado is Voltaire's true ideal. Voltaire the deist offers the reader a blueprint of a model society where deism prevails. Voltaire, the enemy of religious oppression, describes a country where tolerance is practiced. Nevertheless, the emphasis in the treatment of religion in Eldorado is negative rather than positive; its primary function is to satirize religious concepts and practices in the world outside. . . . In Eldorado, men are free in theory: 'tous les hommes sont libres', says the king. They have the right to leave Eldorado, but they have made vows by which they have effectively deprived themselves of this liberty. Moreover, the faith itself of Eldorado rings hollow in its context. [Voltaire scholar] J. G. Weightman suggests that the only way to justify the Eldorado chapters is to suppose that they are really a conscious or unconscious criticism of god. It is easy to thank god continually and to have nothing to ask of him in Eldorado, but it is rather difficult in the world outside, with its earthquakes, wars, and persecutions. The fortunate Eldoradans are not confronted with circumstances that might provoke a crisis in belief, while such circumstances are shown as continually arising in the world outside. It is simplistic to see in the description of the religious beliefs and practices of Eldorado a direct expression of what the author holds to be right.

ABSENCE OF GOVERNMENT INSTITUTIONS

The nature of the political structure of Eldorado is also cited as evidence that the society is Voltaire's ideal as to what

7. What! You mean you don't have any monks to teach and dispute and govern and intrigue and burn people to death who don't agree with them?

mankind should strive toward. Nevertheless, very few details are provided on the actual functioning of the government. The country is ruled by an enlightened monarch who presides over an excellent table and possesses an admirable wit. . . . Institutions such as the court of justice, parliament, and prison are remarkable by their absence. The inhabitants of Eldorado are evidently so virtuous that there is no need for these as there is in the world outside where men are corrupt. Bottiglia explains that there are no courts or prisons on the grounds that the state has withered away under the ideal rule of the beneficent monarch. Surely, however, this is to beg the question. In Eldorado, the citizens seem to have preserved the original innocence that man in the outside world has lost. They can do without institutions that are necessary in a society of fallen individuals. Because evil is non-existent in Eldorado, controls can be dispensed with; the dispensing with controls does not bring about the non-existence of evil. As outside, evil exists, Eldorado cannot provide a genuine model to be striven toward. Only the material achievements of Eldorado are given a limited potential explanation in the palace of sciences with its ten thousand foot long gallery of instruments; the encouragement of scientific inventions has brought about the high living standard.

The institutions and practices of Eldorado—religious, economic, social, and political—serve primarily a satirical purpose, affording the reader with indirect critical insights into the inadequacies of European institutions and practices. Eldorado is a foil to the societies through which Candide has passed and will pass where the Inquisition imposes a reign of terror, and poverty, corruption and oppression are everywhere to be found. Eldorado itself is more of an impossible dream world beset by paradoxes and ambiguities than the true ideal of the perfect state. It is touched by ridicule for its remoteness from reality in a work that insists upon its confrontation and exposes evasions of it through the retreat into metaphysical speculation. Candide and Cacambo, dazzled by what they see in Eldorado, ask each other: 'Quel est donc ce pays. . . inconnu à tout le reste de la terre, et où toute la nature est d'une espèce si différente de la nôtre'?[8] Eldorado is a place where nature, physical and human, is of another kind than in the outside world. It is much more than a mat-

8. What is this place . . . which is unknown to the rest of the world and where the whole nature of things is so different from ours?

ter of surface manners of the inhabitants; it is the very essence of life that is totally different. The opinion proffered by Candide, as Pangloss's pupil, is: 'C'est probablement le pays où tout va bien: *car* il faut absolument qu'il y en ait un de cette espèce'[9] (italics mine). The word *for* should alert the reader to the presence of irony, for it and its synonyms have appeared a number of times already in the work as a part of ironic constructions. . . . In this context, the assertion that Eldorado is the best of all possible worlds is just another proof deduced on the basis of a spurious causality or necessity, and not to be accepted by the reader as the author's opinion on the subject.

The choice of Candide and Cacambo to leave Eldorado has been variously derided by critics of the work as foolish and praised as wise. In the context, the decision is ambiguous in its merits reflecting the ambiguous status of Eldorado itself. On the one hand, Candide and Cacambo would seem to be the object of satire for their incapacity to settle down and remain in the excellent society they have found. The motives given by Candide for departing are hardly worthy of commendation. His desire to be richer than all those around him is certainly deplorable. Even his yearning for reunion with Cunégonde is stripped of much of its potential laudableness by the manner in which he speaks of it; Cunégonde is paralleled casually with 'quelque maîtresse en Europe'[10] that Cacambo undoubtedly would like to rejoin. The additional motives offered by the narrator, restlessness and the longing to boast of things seen in the course of travelling, are also lacking in merit. The narrator's evaluation of their behavior is a condemnation: 'les deux heureux résolurent de ne plus l'être',[11] and is reinforced by the king's chiding remark: 'Vous faites une sottise . . . quand on est passablement quelque part, il faut y rester.'[12] On the other hand, to stay in Eldorado would mean to escape from the evils of the real world rather than to face and deal with them. It is not in man's imperfect nature to find happiness in such a perfect society; the best of all possible worlds is not best suited to man as he is. The best that Candide and Cacambo can do is to take something of Eldorado back with them into the real world. Ironically, what they choose to take seems to be what is of least spiritual value, the gold, silver, and gems that consti-

9. It's probably the place where all goes well, *for* there absolutely must be such a place. 10. some sweetheart back in Europe 11. the two happy men resolved to be happy no longer 12. You're making a great mistake. . . . When one is reasonably content in a place, one ought to stay there.

tute material wealth in the society they have come from. Gradually, these are lost, stolen, and wasted away till almost nothing remains. Enough is left, however, of this earth of Eldorado to purchase the farm where in the end the characters do find a limited contentment.

It is significant that it is after Candide has passed through the utopia of Eldorado that he can at last reject the philosophy of optimism. In approaching, Surinam, confronted with the miserable mutilated Negro, he defines it: 'c'est la rage de soutenir que tout est bien quand on est mal'.[13] He now views optimism as a mania, the delusion of a sick mind. Hereafter, when Eldorado is invoked, it is as the exception that proves the rule that the world is full of imperfections. After listening to the tales of woe of his would-be companions, Candide muses; 'Certainement si tout va bien, c'est dans Eldorado, et non pas dans le reste de la terre'.[14] After his bad experiences in France, Candide is provoked to exclaim: 'J'ai vu des ours dans mon pays; je n'ai vu des hommes que dans le Dorado'.[15] Martin, the pessimist, qualifies his assertion that God has abandoned the world to some evil being: 'j'en excepte toujours Eldorado'.[16] He attempts to prove that there is little virtue and happiness on earth, 'excepté peut-être dans Eldorado, où personne ne pouvait aller'.[17] The Eldorado episode serves to emphasize the sordid qualities of the places to which Candide travels in the succeeding episodes: Surinam, France, England, Venice, Constantinople, the Propontis shores.

All of *Candide* militates against the existence of a best of all possible worlds. The message of the garden of the conclusion is to make the best of the world that is through active work rather than resorting to metaphysics to prove that all that is, is for the best. The satirist is lured by utopia although it is fundamentally at variance with his meaning and method. Voltaire resolves this dilemma and manages to use Eldorado to further his satiric aims rather than confuse them. Eldorado embodies virtues that act to show up the contrasting shortcomings of the world outside. Nevertheless, Eldorado is itself the object of satire; it is treated with ironic detachment and mocked as an impossible dream.

13. it's a mania for insisting that all is well when things are going badly 14. One thing's certain: if all is going well, it's happening in Eldorado and not in the rest of the world. 15. I have seen bears in my own country; I have seen men only in Eldorado. 16. apart from Eldorado, that is 17. except perhaps in Eldorado, where no one can get to

Eldorado as a Vision of a Better World

David Williams

In this article, David Williams, professor of French at
the University of Sheffield, England, argues that Eldorado serves as a standard by which Candide can
measure the rest of his world. This Utopian community serves to show Candide that no matter how bad
things get, there is always something better, somewhere. His experience in Eldorado, Williams maintains, allows him to reject the simplistic ideas of the
Optimists, who claim that everything that happens is
for the best, and to think for himself.

Drawing on well-established conventions of utopic writing,
Voltaire's Eldorado presents a sequence of tableaux in which
familiar ideas on economics, government and religion, typical
of the mid-eighteenth-century Enlightenment, are brought into
rather hazy focus. There is no detailed exploration of any single
issue, and Voltaire took care to invest the episode with an am-
biance of remoteness and isolation. His purpose could have
been primarily satirical. The importance of the land of *gold* in
Candide lies less in its specific details than in its general symbolism as a location of idealism through which Candide must
travel before he can re-engage purposefully with the world as
it is. Eldorado is always in the future—not an *optimum,* but in
its general outlines a progressivist vision of a better world that
challenges the Optimists' claim that perfection is already in
place. Eldorado has nothing of the fixity of the Baron's castle
about it, but is rather in a process of becoming as the emphasis
on dynamic activity suggests. Moreover, Voltaire's picture of Eldoradan life is not entirely free of ambiguities and reservations.

In the scenes in Paraguay, Candide is accompanied by Cacambo, a Figaro-like valet whom he acquired in Cadiz. Cacambo is a South American quadroon by birth with an im-

Excerpted from David Williams, *Voltaire: Candide.* Copyright © 1997 Grant & Cutler
Ltd. Reprinted with permission from Grant & Cutler Ltd. References and footnotes
have been omitted.

pressive list of careers behind him as 'enfant de chœur, sac-
ristain, matelot, moine, facteur, soldat, laquais'.[1] He joins
Jacques and the Old Woman as one of the three main positive
forces in the *conte* [story], and like the Old Woman, but unlike
Jacques, he is a survivor. He takes the initiative, and facilitates
Candide's transition from the world of abstractions, illusions
and nostalgia to the world of action and reality. After the
strange encounter with the Oreillons in Chapter 16, in which
the Rousseauist thesis about the natural goodness of man had
been tested and found wanting, Candide and Cacambo arrive,
thanks to Cacambo's resourcefulness, at the borders of Eldorado. The pace of the narrative decelerates sharply in Chapters 17 and 18, and the effect is to generate a mood of reflec-
tive calm. These two chapters are further distanced from the
rest of the text by a style of writing in which the usual mis-
chievous edge and linguistic *brio* [enthusiastic vigor] are no-
ticeably subdued. Nevertheless, the Eldoradan episode is not
a totally self-contained interlude. This is not just a snap-shot
of Voltaire's ideal state, unrelated either to what precedes it or
to what happens next. Eldorado interlocks with the rest of the
tale, and has a particularly close bearing on interpretations of
the tale's conclusion.

DESCRIPTION OF ELDORADO

After their narrow escape from the *mise en broche* at the
hands of the Oreillons, Candide and Cacambo are temporarily disorientated and dispirited, the world seemingly offering
them only a choice between degrees of unpleasantness. The
path to Eldorado is not easily negotiated, but while the landscape is wild and dangerous, its hostility to hopeful and determined travellers is not an insuperable obstacle to
progress. For the first time in *Candide* nature is benevolent.
Wild fruits sustain them, and after a month they end up on
the banks of an unknown river lined with coconut-trees 'qui
soutinrent leur vie et leurs espérances',[2] luck and their own
resourcefulness having helped them on their way. The account of their arrival is charged with symbolism, though entirely free from any hint of the fabulous, the miraculous or
the fantastic that contemporary readers might have expected. . . . The description of Eldorado itself is not entirely
a figment of Voltaire's imagination, but it has an overlay of

1. choir-boy, sexton, sailor, monk, commercial agent, soldier, and lackey 2. which kept
both them and their hopes alive

symbolic features that crystallise more clearly when compared to other parts of the text, especially Chapter 1 and Chapter 30.

Unlike the 'parc' in the Baron's castle, and unlike Pococuranté's garden, 'le pays était cultivé pour le plaisir comme pour le besoin: partout l'utile était agréable'.[3] Handsome men and beautiful women ride in splendid carriages drawn by 'moutons rouges' (llamas?), capable of outpacing the fastest horse. Eldorado is a place of spaciousness and 'filtered luminosity' radiating benevolence, beneficence and harmony. The light of Eldorado casts an ironic shadow over Candide and Cacambo, who can only observe the scene with uncomprehending European eyes, and evaluate it in the light of unworthy European values. One thing does become clear to Candide, however. The Panglossian assumption of an *optimum* in Westphalia is now definitely vulnerable: 'Voilà pourtant [...] un pays qui vaut mieux que la Westphalie'.[4]

INVERSIONS

The discovery of Eldorado comes at the point where both the old and the new worlds have been found wanting. Following conventions of utopic fiction, Eldorado offers a polarised mirror-image of the values and attitudes of outside 'normality'. Iconic symbols of wealth—precious metals and stones—have no value here beyond the utilitarian. This Eldorado is not a metal-based economy in spite of its name, its wealth being based on what is produced, an echo perhaps of Voltaire's physiocratic sympathies that will be heard again at the end of the tale. Children, dressed in gold- and silver-emblazoned clothes, play marbles with priceless jewels. They are not the royal princes that European logic assumes them to be, but merely 'petits gueux' ["little urchins"]. Their indifference to the 'value' of their toys is matched only by the greed of the travellers in wishing to pocket them. The opening scene invites the reader to reconsider the relationship of wealth to happiness.

Another inn scene then takes place, its pleasures contrasting sharply with the dangers, deceits and disasters encountered in other inns. Here there are no predators, philosophers or vagabonds, only honest people doing useful

3. the land had been cultivated as much to give pleasure as to serve a need 4. This, on the other hand . . . is something of an improvement on Westphalia.

work: 'pour la plupart des marchands et des voituriers'.[5] Unlike the meal offered to Candide by the Bulgar recruiters,
with which this scene has a carefully configured binary relationship, the acceptance of food does not spring a trap. Attempts by the travellers to pay for the meal with the diamonds just picked up in the street results only in laughter
and the explanation that meals are subsidised in Eldoradan
inns in the interests of trade, one of the few references to a
specific example of an Eldoradan government policy. Trade
and the values of a merchant class, already exemplified by
Jacques, are clearly intended as key features of Eldoradan
life, although how mercantilism operates in practical terms,
and to what purpose in a country without currency or profit
motive, is not explored.

The social and economic disorientation of Candide and
Cacambo is accentuated by a pointedly unwarranted apol-
ogy from the innkeeper for the frugality of the meal, and the
paradoxical assurance that the travellers will find a higher
quality of service elsewhere in Eldorado. Again they reflect
on where they could be, Candide noting that it was almost
certainly the place where all really was well: 'Et, quoi qu'en
dît maître Pangloss, je me suis souvent aperçu que tout allait
mal en Westphalie'.[6] Enlightenment comes from a wise
'vieillard', one of the standard tropes in Voltairean fiction.
The conventional master-servant relationship between Candide and Cacambo now changes temporarily to one based
on talent rather than class. Elsewhere in the tale Candide
seems to have no linguistic difficulties, but with the exception of Spanish, the New World languages of the Oreillons
and the Eldoradans defeat him. Cacambo knows how to
speak Peruvian, the language of Eldorado, and this unex-
plained linguistic advantage (and why should it be explained in a *conte*?) enables him to seize the initiative in the
conversation with the Old Man. In due course, the Candide-
Cacambo, relationship will consolidate an important *leitmo-
tif* in the later stages of the tale relating to friendship, and the
value of shared human feelings and experience.

In Chapter 18 the Old Man tells of the origins of Eldorado
in the 'étonnantes révolutions du Pérou',[7] and in an account
that bears a passing resemblance to Montesquieu's story of

5. tradesmen and wagoners for the most part 6. And whatever Maître Pangloss might
have said, I often observed that everything went rather badly in Westphalia. 7. extraordinary upheavals . . . in Peru

the Troglodytes in Letters 11–14 of the *Lettres persanes*, the travellers learn that Eldorado is a kingdom which the Incas abandoned in order to pursue foreign conquests, an unwise policy resulting in their slaughter at the hands of the Spanish. Learning the lesson of this experience, the Eldoradans have severed their links with the world to secure their survival. They have turned their backs on evil, but in contrast to the Thunder-ten-Tronckh situation, they are quite aware of evil's presence in the world, and of their vulnerability to it. The policy of withdrawal behind closed frontiers imposes constraints on freedom that mysteriously carry with them the consent of the people, 'et c'est ce qui nous a conservé notre innocence et notre félicité'.[8] This policy, together with the natural protection afforded by the surrounding terrain, gives Eldorado the air of a mental and physical fortress existing in self-imposed isolation from the mainstream of human affairs, neither importing nor exporting goods, people or ideas.

RELIGION, GOVERNMENT, AND SCIENCE

The travellers are particularly curious about religion, always for Voltaire the litmus test of a society's health. Candide and Cacambo assume wrongly that there is no religion in Eldorado, and the Old Man's response allows the issue of sectarian strife to be raised obliquely. Cacambo presses the Old Man for further details with what the latter can only regard as ["strange questions"] that only 'les gens de votre monde'[9] could pose. Most of the information about this aspect of Eldoradan civil life reflects Voltaire's views on the merits of the deistic ethic, and contains few surprises except perhaps for the baffling reference to worship of the deity as being a nocturnal activity. There are no sects, no dogma, no professional clergy, no superstition, no intolerance, no *auto-da-fés* [burning of heretics during the Inquisition], and above all no religious meddling in political matters. Nothing is asked of the deity, prayers consisting only of giving thanks for blessings received. Most important of all, the infectious 'rage' of fanaticism has not touched Eldorado. . . .

The organisation and administration of civil affairs are not elaborated in any great detail, although a long conversation is reported to have taken place on 'la forme du gou-

8. and that's how we've managed to remain innocent and happy 9. people from your part of the world

vernement, sur les mœurs, sur les femmes, sur les spectacles publics, sur les arts'.[10] The King of Eldorado is a *roi-philosophe* [philosopher king], whose portrait contrasts sharply with that of the King of the Bulgars. In the scene describing the court reception for Candide the royal guards turn out to be pretty girls who receive the strangers in extravagantly sumptuous style: 'les conduisirent aux bains, les vêtirent de robes d'un tissu de duvet de colibri'.[11] The King of Eldorado confounds Candide further when it becomes clear that the abasement of commoners before royalty is not practised, and that it is not necessary in Eldorado to crawl on one's knees or lick the ground in the presence of kings. There is no trace of the cold remoteness of the faceless Bulgar autocrat in this king who greets his guests as equals. Nor will this king form part of the ragged chorus-line of failed monarchs that Candide will meet in Venice in Chapter 26.

Much of the discursive undertow of the Eldoradan episode concerns power relations and the attitude that should be taken towards superior beings, whether gods or kings. In Eldorado authority figures are respected, not for the fear that they instil, but for the feelings of natural affection that their beneficence inspires. Beyond that the nature of the King of Eldorado's authority, and the extent of his power over his subjects, remain a matter for speculation. The text simply signals that the king is an enlightened monarch governing by popular consent, and that monarchical rule in Eldorado is a uniting force for social harmony and cohesion. Despite the egalitarian ethos, however, the social structure is still clearly pyramidic. Power is not exercised in an overtly autocratic manner, but covertly the authority of the few governs the lives of the rest, albeit benevolently. The discreet nature of kingly power resurfaces when the two travellers wish to leave Eldorado.

In their tour of the city, Candide and Cacambo learn that there are no courts of justice, no *parlement* or other legislative buildings, and no prisons. Law and order simply exist. Citizens of Eldorado do not commit crimes, or go to war, or display selfish, socially harmful behaviour. Human nature in Eldorado has been purged of wickedness. How this has been achieved is not clear, although Voltaire raises by impli-

10. the form of government there, on local customs, on women, public entertainment, and the arts 11. they escorted them to the baths, and dressed them in robes of hummingbird down.

cation Rousseau's link between the transformation of society and the regeneration of the individual. The civilising effects of art and culture possibly have a role to play here too. Certainly the arts and the sciences are in a healthier state than they prove to be in Paris and Venice.

The vigorous, uncensored pursuit of knowledge can be inferred from the existence of a 'palais des sciences' with its exhibition of scientific instruments. Science in Eldorado compares favourably with the frivolities that pass for scientific research at the Bordeaux Academy. Eldoradan scientists share and communicate the civilising benefits of their knowledge, a far cry from the arcane pursuits of their counterparts in Europe. Music and architecture combine harmo-

---

THE QUOTABLE VOLTAIRE

Voltaire is widely known for being witty and wise, with a flip comment for any occasion. Many of his most famous quotations and excerpts from his works are contained in a great number of treasuries, though their specific sources are rarely given. Here are some of his most famous observations:

All the known world, excepting only savage nations, is governed by books.

Providence has given us hope and sleep as a compensation for the many cares of life.

My prayer to God is a very short one: "Oh Lord, make my enemies ridiculous!" God has granted it.

Is there anyone so wise as to learn by the experience of others?

What a heavy burden is a name that has become too famous.

If there were no God, it would be necessary to invent him.

History is only a record of crimes and misfortunes.

Ideas are like beards: men do not have them until they grow up.

Nature has always had more force than education.

The infinitely little have a pride infinitely great.

Many are destined to reason wrongly; others, not to reason at all; and others, to persecute those who do reason.

Satire lies about men while they live and eulogy lies about them when they die.

In general, the art of government consists in taking as much money as possible from one class of citizens to give to the other.

niously to produce beauty and pleasure. There is no reference to literature or the other arts, and metaphysics and philosophy are naturally ignored. As with the countryside surrounding the city-state, the social landscape is also
cultivated with a view to making ["the useful also agreeable"].

THE NEED TO MOVE ON

From the standpoint of characterisation, the Eldoradans
come to life only as part of a homogeneous collectivity. Their
group portrait is that of a communal self, and lacks the
strong colours and raw vitality of other crowds in *Candide*.
While the Eldoradans have no problem with boredom, *ennui*
might well be a danger for the two travellers, should they
choose to stay. The word *happiness* is never mentioned, but
the Eldoradans seem to be happy, or at least they perceive
themselves to be happy, which is perhaps all that matters.
The question of self-perception, and its relationship to self-
determination, will arise again in Chapter 30. Eldorado is
the gold standard by which to measure the inadequacies of
the present and the possibilities for the future. It points back-
wards to Westphalia and forwards to Candide's garden in
Turkey, a crucially important staging post in the hero's journey, but not his destination.

As the episode draws to a close, and its possible purpose
as a symbol of human aspiration has been served, narrative
imperatives take over. Candide must move on. He and Cacambo are representatives of unregenerated humanity, and
after a month Candide finds that the delights of the city of
gold start to pall, reminding us that the values of *Candide*
are not always Candide's. Assimilation into the Eldoradan
communal self holds few attractions for Candide, to his discredit perhaps. However, his reservation raises intriguing
question marks: 'Si nous restons ici, nous n'y serons que
comme les autres'.[12]

Ambiguities aside, the Eldoradan experience has been on
the whole educative and beneficial, and Candide returns to
his quest strengthened and more resolute than before. The
prospect of reunion with Cunégonde is no longer a vague
dream but a practical proposition for which Eldorado has
opened up new possibilities, not the least of which are those

12. If we stay on here, we'll simply be the same as everyone else.

that result from the possession of Eldoradan ["riches"]. Cacambo is persuaded (not ordered) to leave with him, and
with their joint decision to return to Europe, 'les deux
heureux résolurent de ne plus l'être'.[13] In the end, Eldorado
has offered them pleasure but not true happiness, sanctuary
but not purpose. The King wishes them to stay, but understands their desire to leave. He does not impose his will, but
offers them wise advice instead: 'Vous faites une sottise [...]
je sais bien que mon pays est peu de chose mais, quand on
est passablement quelque part, il faut y rester'.[14] We must
wait for Chapter 30 before we see a Candide ready and able
to see any wisdom in that statement. Meanwhile, the travellers are free to go: 'tous les hommes sont libres'.[15]

Leaving Eldorado proves to be as difficult as entering it,
but the King commissions three thousand scientists to create an ingenious machine to ensure a safe exit, a testimony
to the benefits of co-operative endeavour and collaboration
that provides another link with Chapter 30. Accompanied by
a hundred 'red sheep' loaded down with Eldoradan gold and
precious stones, the 'deux vagabonds' take their leave. Any
authorial reproof implied by their new designation as
'vagabonds' is short-lived. Suggestions of greed and other
morally dubious motives soon disappear, although the impression is left that neither Candide nor Cacambo was actually worthy of permanent residence in the city of gold.

On the other hand, significant changes for the better have
taken place in the hero. From now on he will be able to
break the freedom-denying links in the chain of cause-and-
effect that has ordered his life in the pre-Eldoradan world of
Optimism. Thoughts of Eldorado will not fade, moreover. In
addition to their practical usefulness as living banks, the red
sheep will perpetuate symbolically the presence of Eldorado
in the rest of the *conte*. They will provide a splash of colour
in the darkness, and remind Candide that all is never for the
best, that there is always a better world, that solutions to
some problems can be found, and that the human struggle
against evil is not entirely futile. After Eldorado the paraly-
sis of Optimism lifts a little; progress becomes a possibility,
and the will to act manifests itself, freedom to act being assured by the contents of the bags carried by the red sheep.

13. the two happy men resolved to be happy no longer 14. You're making a great mistake
. . . I know my country isn't up to much, but when one is reasonably content in a place,
one ought to stay there. 15. All men are free.

A Garden of Hope

William F. Bottiglia

Although it is just one of three gardens in the concluding chapter, William F. Bottiglia asserts that Candide's garden symbolizes humankind's best hope for
productive occupation. Bottiglia examines Cacambo's
and the old Turk's gardens, exposing the progression
from individuality to family unit, and finally shows
us how Candide's garden represents a group functioning together in a model society in which every-
body has a purpose. Bottiglia, of the Massachusetts
Institute of Technology, has published, among other
works, "Voltaire's *Candide:* Analysis of a Classic."

The fact that Voltaire is attacking optimism does not mean
that he is embracing its opposite. If he rejects optimism, he
does so not only on the ground of its metaphysical bluff but
also [in the words of critic Norman L. Torrey] on account of
its "devitalizing agency," its discouraging fatalism. It is true
that he treats Martin much more sympathetically than Pangloss, partly for polemical reasons, partly because the former's philosophy does less violence to the facts of life. But
his handling of Martin in Chapter XXX shows plainly that
pessimism does not triumph at the end. The author himself
refers to Martin's principles as "detestable"—a valuation
completely ignored by all critics who favor a pessimistic interpretation of the Conclusion. What is more, when Martin
states that man was born to live "in the convulsions of anxiety, or in the lethargy of boredom," Candide *disagrees*, although he is not yet ready to voice a positive opinion of his
own. Later, in the ripeness of time, it is Candide who makes
the great affirmation, while Martin, like Pangloss, merely
falls into line with an echoing judgment. Thus the pessimist
and the optimist lose their respective identities to merge
with their former disciple, now suddenly matured into the
meliorist. In sum, Voltaire carefully shuns *both* extremes. In-

Excerpted from William F. Bottiglia, *Voltaire: A Collection of Critical Essays* (New
Jersey: Prentice-Hall, Inc., 1968).

deed, if, after his sustained assault on optimistic fatalism, he had concluded by adopting *pessimistic* fatalism, he would have perpetrated a glaring non sequitur, he would have killed the point of his tale, destroyed his case, lost the battle he had set out to win—the battle to preserve the moral initiative for his deistic humanism. . . .

EXAMINING THE GARDENS

The first of the three gardens in Chapter XXX is Cacambo's. *Physically, it is the same garden as Candide's.* On this point [critic René] Pomeau comments: "The survivors of the tale had been settled there for some time without knowing it. A profound lesson: all men are already in the only possible paradise. It is quite simply up to them to realize it." Voltaire's full meaning is richer than Pomeau suggests. Cacambo's garden and Candide's are physically identical, but the one precedes and the other follows the dawning of wisdom through consultation of the dervish and the old Turk. Before that dawning Cacambo works alone and curses his fate; after it the entire group finds happiness in co-operative labor. The example had been set for both him and Candide by the Eldoradans. Neither, however, was then mature enough to appreciate the contentment that comes from socially purposeful collaboration. Torrey says of Candide's garden that it reveals a Voltaire at "the bottom of his emotional curve." More accurately, it is Cacambo's garden which represents such a depression of spirits, along with the attitudes of Martin, of Pococurante, and of Candide at Surinam.

The second of the three gardens in Chapter XXX is the old Turk's. Here the author has blended *overstatement* with *duplicity,* hammering home the former—"I know nothing about it," "I have never known," "I know absolutely nothing," "I never make inquiries"—in order to prepare the reader for the latter—"I content myself with sending the fruits of the garden I cultivate to market there." The old Turk is no rude, untutored peasant. He is head of a well-bred, hard-working family, and he is a master of literary utterance, climaxing his series of incisive, elegantly turned observations with the magnificent aphorism: "work keeps away from us three great evils: boredom, vice, and want." If such a person insists that it is best to remain rigidly indifferent, even ignorant, respecting the world, Voltaire is soberly implying: 1) that men of good will should turn their backs on public abominations in a gesture of philosophic disdain; 2) that they should seek positions wherein they can maximize their personal safety and provide the fullest possible scope for their self-determination; 3) that they should work to banish the basic evils of boredom, vice, and want by producing for the market of the world. Once again there is an effect of shrinkage. The *philosophe* must dissociate himself from all corrupt governments, since they would embrace him only to stifle him; and he must withdraw to where he is secure from their abuses of power. But there is also countermovement, with potentially explosive overtones. After so much ironic emphasis on the helplessness of the individual, Voltaire now seriously suggests that men have a certain freedom of action. He further suggests that they can exert an influence for the better on the world at large, not by overt participation in its political affairs, but by supplying it with nutriment, as well as by setting a good example. Considering the heavy exaggeration of the old Turk's opening remarks, his traits of character, the many values directly or indirectly affirmed throughout the tale as worth salvaging, and its calculated symbolism, what critic would be so rash as to propose that the nutriment being supplied is restricted to food? The fruits of the old Turk's garden include more than legumes; they include intellectual pabulum.

A PROGRESSION TO COMMUNITY

A comparison of Candide's garden with those of Cacambo and the old Turk reveals *a deliberate progression from lone individual to family circle to small model group;* also, in all three (explicitly in the first two, implicitly in the third), the practical enterprise of selling their produce in the metropolitan market. The progression is objectively there, and it has profound implications. It proves that the effect of shrinkage is accompanied and balanced by an effect of expansion. The former, however, fulfills its function within the limits of the tale. The latter projects beyond those limits. The Conclusion of *Candide* is an ending with a vista. The vista is neither infinite nor insipidly roseate, but it does hold promise of solid humanistic advancement, of augmentative and ameliorative evolution in the direction of Eldoradan values. The pattern of the final chapter, no less eloquent than its language, informs the alert and sensitive reader that Candide's garden is not a terminus, but a commencement. Animated by an inherent dynamism, it will outgrow itself—*provided* its inhabitants continue to work together and are spared a natural catastrophe. This vista suffices by itself to destroy the Fundamentalist interpretation, for the future of the garden must entail something more than the growing of bigger and better vegetables.

As for interpretations which dwell on "selfish indifference" and "the doctrine of minding one's own business," they are refuted by Voltaire's own words. Candide's garden is co-operatively cultivated by "the entire little community." Pomeau contends that Pangloss constitutes an exception: "He alone escapes the final reformation of the little community. . . . Still 'arguing without working,' he remains imperturbably Pangloss, the man who is nothing but talk." The text of the tale, however, makes Pangloss a member of "the *entire* little community," and therefore one of its active workers. Moreover, it represents him as relapsing only "sometimes" into otiose [futile] speculation. Like his companions, then, he becomes socially useful in accordance with deistic doctrine. But social utility is not confined to the "little community.". . .The sale of produce establishes a connection with the big city—a connection wherein it is the small model group which influences the world, and not the other way around. But if the garden is to be understood symbolically as well as literally, then its yield must be such as to affect not only the bodies but also the minds of men.

In this regard it is a point of key importance that *Candide's garden involves more than gardening.* Each member of the group puts his particular talents to use. Cunégonde becomes a pastry cook, Paquette embroiders, the old woman takes care of the linen, Friar Giroflée does the carpentry. Cacambo presumably continues to grow vegetables and to market them in the metropolis. What of the remaining three members? Voltaire uses the others to illustrate very concretely the beginnings of specialized labor in a civilized society. Why does he say nothing specific about the work of Candide, Pangloss, and Martin? Several times in the course of the final chapter he focuses attention on them as *the intellectual subgroup* of the "little community." They undoubtedly help in the physical garden, but they, too, must have a specialty. Both Martin and Candide, applying the lesson taught by the dervish, discourage Pangloss from speculating about ultimates. That does not, however, preclude the composition and dissemination of socially useful literature. The activities of this civilization-in-miniature not only go beyond literal gardening to the extent of including carpentry, laundering, embroidery, and baking; they also include the life of the mind concentrated on the spreading of utilitarian knowledge. To argue the opposite would, of course, be absurd. Does Candide achieve mature wisdom by repudiating the life of the mind and degenerating into a brute fellah? Voltaire's silence respecting the intellectual activity of Candide's model group is not a denial of its existence. Once again, his patterns powerfully convey his full meaning. I have just mentioned the pattern of the intellectual subgroup. There is, in addition, the pattern of *the disingenuous stance.* The duplicity of the old Turk's family circle prepares that of Candide's little band. . . .

THE SUPERIORITY OF PRODUCTIVITY

There is still another pattern which contributes in an important way to the elucidation of Voltaire's closing message. *Voltaire has Candide state his conclusion, not once, but twice, the second time with dilated meaning.* In good music the restatement of a theme after an intervening development constitutes something more than a mechanical repetition. It enables the listener to hear the theme with a new understanding of its meaning, to appreciate it in a richer perspective. And so with Candide's conclusion. The first time he makes his affirmation, it is already charged with considerable significance. It chokes off Pangloss's pedantic prolixity, opposing the Deed to the Word. It dramatically underlines the antithesis between those who bloody the earth and those who cultivate it. It proclaims the immeasurable superiority of productivity to power politics. It invites to reflection on the values preached and practised by the old Turk and his family. And it casts a fitful light over the long, fantastic road traveled by Candide and his companions. But all this is not yet fully clear. The author has said too much and moved too swiftly for the reader to be able to absorb the final wisdom in one abrupt, climactic judgment. With great tactical skill he goes on to the elaboration of his theme. First he varies it. The variation sounded by Pangloss harks back to the beginning of the tale and, with consummate irony, to the beginning of the Scriptural Revelation. That voiced by Martin picks up the dervish's message and beautifully fuses the effect of shrinkage with that of expansion.

The effect of expansion, however, still remains to be clarified. Having stated and varied his theme, Voltaire now proceeds to develop it. He shows us the little band purposefully hustling and bustling about its business, achieving co-operative contentment, serving as a miniature model for the world, and seeking to help make the world's business more like its own. The picture is much clearer now, provided the reader has been alert to the stylistic and structural devices which the master-storyteller is dynamically interweaving as he approaches the end of his story. The end takes the form of a summation in two contrasting speeches. That of Pangloss, a parody of periodic eloquence and a caricature of optimistic dialectic, nevertheless manages to provide a rapid review of several major motifs and episodes: namely, both the intellectual and the sentimental aspects of optimism, the inhumanity of man to man, religious fanaticism, the aimlessness of the South-American adventure, the visit by special dispensation to Eldorado, and the worthlessness of unearned wealth. This review rings a number of changes on social unproductiveness, while reminding us of its ideal opposite. Candide's response, quietly tolerant of his comrade's occasional aberrations, pointed, terse, lapidary, reaffirms the theme of productivity, which this time, because of the intervening development, renews, enriches, deepens, and broadens the meaning of the garden. The restatement flashes both back and forward. It is a wondrous epitome of the tale's wisdom, coined neither for mere show nor for mere contemplation, but for *use.* . . .

THE UNCERTAIN FATE OF THE COMMUNITY

Pomeau raises the interesting and very important question of how the garden is socially and administratively organized. "Good humor," he states, "prevents the problem of social relationships from being posed. No leadership, no subordination in 'the little community.' Voltaire, easy-to-get-along-with fellow that he is, assumes that work organizes itself. . . ." Since it is Candide who makes the big decision while the others simply accept it, and since it is he who has the last word, I think it plain enough that he has now become the leader of the group. Moreover, Voltaire is under no obligation to do more than start the group on its way at the end. The rest is a matter of time, effort, intelligence, and good will. Nor must it be forgotten that the general direction of possible development may be inferred from the ideal society in the Eldorado episode. Voltaire definitely knows that it is men who organize work, and that in due course, if things go reasonably well, equality before the law will be preserved, but a social and economic hierarchy will take shape.

The nature of Candide's garden makes it dependent on those who work in it, to be sure, but also, as already noted, on the lucky avoidance of physical disasters, and, finally, on its security against destruction by hostile governments. There is nothing automatic or certain about it, then. Its existence is precarious. It is a beautiful but fragile thing. Yet it represents man's best hope—indeed, his only hope *as* man; and it is therefore the only thing with which he has a human right to occupy himself.

One more point: Voltaire's conception of the garden is plural. Wherever a few persons gather in the name of social productivity, a garden comes into existence. Given enough of these developing, setting an example, and influencing the world, a global metagarden is conceivable. Conceivable, that is, as Eldorado is conceivable; but Voltaire is too much the realist to regard a global metagarden as fully realizable on this "globule." It is sufficient for him that men should move toward it, no matter how modestly, in attestation of their higher humanity.

The great mass of internal evidence proves that the meaning of the Conclusion is complex but not obscure, and that Voltaire does not end by abandoning the world to the wicked after flaying them with his verbal lash. He ends by affirming that social productivity of any kind at any level constitutes the good life, that there are limits within which man must be satisfied to lead the good life, but that within these he has a very real chance of achieving both private contentment and public progress.

Mythical and Symbolic Gardens

Patrick Henry

Patrick Henry argues that Westphalia and Eldorado are mythical in nature, with strong parallels to the Garden of Eden in the Old Testament, while Candide's garden at the end of the tale symbolizes his growth and maturity. Henry, a professor of French language and literature at Whitman College who has published works on Voltaire as well as French authors Camus and Montaigne, shows how Voltaire uses the gardens to illustrate Candide's progression from innocence to experience.

In the following pages, the Westphalian garden of chapter one, the garden of Eldorado of chapters seventeen and eighteen and the final garden, that of Candide, will be examined. These three gardens establish the central mythical design of the tale and are so clearly symmetrical that they form a solid framework within which the mythical possibilities of the text can begin to be perceived and ultimately elucidated. . . .

THE WESTPHALIAN GARDEN: EDENIC INNOCENCE

The Westphalian garden of chapter one of *Candide* seems to have a two-fold function. It serves, first of all, to describe, on the broadest mythical plane, the perfection of the beginnings of things, the original golden age of the past where one observes a pre-established vertical harmony between men and gods. Here we are in the realm of mythical time or sacred history, or perhaps of no time, for in the Christian tradition from Augustine onward time begins with the Fall. For purposes of consistency, the time of myth—to be distinguished from profane or historical time—will here be identified as sacred time. . . . On the psychological level, of course, this is the paradise of youth, the cosy garden of childhood security.

This universe is characterized by order, stability, peace, harmony, and solidity. The Westphalian garden follows the traditional *topos* [place] of garden as natural *locus amœnus* [lovely place] and place of eternal summer. On the Christian mythical level, one finds here a parody of the book of Genesis that symbolically represents the paradisiac age of prelapsarian man. In this terrestrial paradise, Candide is Adam before the Fall, Cunégonde, Eve and the Baron Thunder-ten-tronckh, who rules the universe of his creation, a grotesque exemplification of the Old Testament God of thunder and lightning. This garden is an *axis mundi*, a meeting place of heaven, earth and hell for it is common belief that 'Adam was created at the centre of the earth, at the same spot where the Cross of Christ was later to be set up.' It is therefore a centre, a sacred space and a zone of absolute reality where God and man have direct communication.

After the depiction of the state of man before the Fall, we come upon a parody of the expulsion from paradise. Just as in the book of Genesis where Adam and Eve are driven from Eden for having eaten of the tree of knowledge, the state of innocence in *Candide* is also the state of ignorance and Cunégonde, after witnessing the scene between Paquette and Pangloss, returns to the château 'toute remplie du désir d'être savante'.[1] Again, as in the Bible, it is woman who tempts man—'elle lui prit innocemment la main''[2]—but here Candide, who succumbs instantaneously, is alone driven from the terrestrial paradise 'à grands coups de pied dans le derrière'.[3]

The fall into time, or more precisely into profane time, is immediately and jarringly rendered when, after the traditional eternal summer of the paradisiac age, Candide finds himself in a place where 'la neige tombait à gros flocons.'[4] As Candide steps not only from sacred to profane time but from sacred to profane place, the relationship of man to the universe changes from an 'I-thou' to an 'I-it' relationship, for Candide finds himself in a hostile world where he must fend for himself. We have indeed moved from cosmos to chaos. This expulsion from Eden is an eschatological myth for it is not only a beginning but an end of an age. It is interesting to note at this juncture that [German philosopher Immanuel] Kant judged the destruction of the paradisiac state a preliminary condition for the discovery of intelligence.

1. filled with the desire to be a scientist 2. innocently she took his hand 3. with a number of hefty kicks up the backside 4. the snow fell in large flakes

From chapters two to four, Candide's temporal reflections are distinguished by nostalgic thoughts of the past age of paradise, what [author Miscea] Eliade would call 'primordiality nostalgia'. Voltaire's hero is haunted by the memories of a lost fatherland where he enjoyed youth, innocence and shelter. These reflections keep him chained to the past and the impossible dream of returning to the structured universe of childhood security. In chapter four, however, he happens upon his former tutor, now ravaged with syphilis: 'pourquoi n'êtes-vous plus dans le plus beau des châteaux?',[5] he asks. Pangloss responds, and Candide faints at the news, that the château has been destroyed: 'il n'est pas resté pierre sur pierre, pas une grange, pas un mouton, pas un canard, pas un arbre'.[6] This marks the definitive demolition of the terrestrial paradise of the past for the château symbolized the pre-established vertical harmony of the structured universe of the prelapsarian state. Candide's dream of belonging to a coherently structured universe has been shattered along with the château. The symbols of solidity, harmony and permanence have already been metamorphosed into those of transience, discord and chaos.

With the reunion with Cunégonde in chapter eight and the separation of the two lovers in chapter thirteen, Candide's temporal preoccupations shift to the future and the possibility of a return to the golden age. Voltaire now explicitly parodies the literature of quest and the archetype of the voyage. Candide, of course, is not named Candide for nothing and now, knowing that the best of all possible worlds behind him is in ashes, he assumes that one must exist in front of him in time. He sets out therefore to find the golden age and the return to sacred time and place. This is the significance of the Eldorado incident that occurs at the centre of the tale.

ELDORADO: THE GOLDEN AGE

While the entrance to Eldorado contains many aspects of myth, it seems to emphasize the difficulty of passage. The traditional road to the centre is always fraught with perils and the path leading to Eldorado is no exception. A series of seemingly insurmountable obstacles are put in the path of Candide as he and Cacambo continue the journey unaware

5. Why are you no longer in the most beautiful of castles? 6. not one stone remains standing on another. Not a single barn, or sheep, or duck, or tree is left.

of their imminent arrival in the country of gold. . . . Their horses die of fatigue and they live for a month on wild fruits before they decide to drift down a nearby river in a canoe. . . . The mountains, the narrow passageway, the inaccessibility, isolation and presence of obstacles all suggest the difficulty of passage common to the entrance to an *axis mundi*, or centre of the world. For the archaic mentality and for *homo religiosus* [religious man] of all ages, the act of climbing or ascending symbolizes the way towards 'the absolute reality'. Whether it be the symbolism of steps, ladders, ropes or mountains, ascending represents the passage from one mode of being to another and with this passage 'a cessation of the profane human condition . . . a breaking of the ontological plane . . . a passing from the unreal to reality' [in the words of Eliade].

The passage from the country of the Oreillons in particular and from all the countries passed through by Candide to Eldorado is literally and metaphorically an ascent to a realm of being physically, culturally, socially and spiritually elevated. When they arrive there, the pace of the narrative slows down to allow the two travellers and the reader sufficient time to visit 'l'ancienne patrie des Incas'[7] and to experience the harmony, simplicity, order and luxury of Eldorado. What first catches the reader's attention, after fifteen chapters of slaughter, pestilence, and death that reflect the powers of darkness, is the proliferation of images of light. Bright objects abound in the text: gold, emeralds, rubies, 'des plats d'une espèce de cristal de roche',[8] 'des vases de diamant',[9] and scattered all over the country and therefore present everywhere is the famous 'matière brillante' shining with particular lustre. There are no prisons, *parlements* or courts of justice here while the arts and sciences are seemingly practised. In addition, the public buildings 'élevès jusqu'aux nues'[10] are structures, like church doors, that open vertically and along with the previously mentioned 'voûte de rochers . . . qui s'élevaient jusqu'au ciel'[11] suggest the mythical time of direct physical interaction between men and gods.

The passage to Eldorado constitutes a veritable ontological mutation but one that the hero experiences only as a witness. Unlike the same phenomenon in most myths, the

7. the former homeland of the Incas 8. dishes made of a kind of rock-crystal 9. diamond goblets 10. raised to the skies 11. vault of fearsome-looking rocks that reached high into the sky

agent himself is not transformed. Candide experiences a transition from one realm of being to another but does not partake of it. This is why he is so obviously out of place in Eldorado. The narrator refers to Candide and Cacambo as 'nos deux hommes de l'autre monde'[12] and 'les deux étrangers'[13]; the host exclaims: 'nous voyons bien que vous êtes des étrangers'. Candide's vanity, restlessness and rapacity dearly distinguish him from the inhabitants who are content to live without ambition, have no taste for gold and have vowed to spend their lives in Eldorado. Candide is quite correct when he tells Cacambo that they are in a country 'où toute la nature est d'une espèce si différente de la [leur]'.[14]

At first blush, inasmuch as the inhabitants have preserved their 'innocence et . . . félcité,'[15] Eldorado may appear as another parody of the garden of Eden. I would like to suggest, nonetheless, that despite many essential similarities between Eden and Eldorado, they remain distinct from one another. In the first place, we find in Eldorado 'le palais des sciences'[16] whereas in Eden the tree of knowledge bore the forbidden fruit. Sciences, carriages and machines did not exist *ab origine* [from origin (of mankind)]and their presence in Eldorado indicates that we are no longer in the *illud tempus* [enjoyable time] of the beginning of things. In the strictest sense of the term, therefore, Voltaire's utopia is not a parody of prelapsarian man. In the first garden of our text, we found, for example, the traditional garden as natural *locus amœnus*; here, however, we have the garden as man-made *locus amœnus*. Unlike the first garden that parodied the golden age of the past, Eldorado represents a somewhat secularized mythical re-enactment of the return of the golden age.

Despite its secular aspects, however, a pre-established vertical harmony still exists between the inhabitants and God. In their ordered universe, there is no longer a direct physical communion between God and man but there is still direct communication between the creator and his creatures. They all practise the same religion of adoration and thanksgiving. When Candide asks the old man how they pray to God in Eldorado, he replies: 'Nous ne le prions point . . . nous n'avons rien à lui demander; il nous a donné tout ce qu'il nous faut; nous le remercions sans cesse'.[17] This is

12. our two men from the other world 13. we can see you're strangers 14. where the whole nature of things is so different from ours 15. innocence . . .and happiness 16. Palace of Science 17. We don't pray to God . . . We have nothing to ask him for. He has given us all we need, and we never cease to thank him.

the universe of cosmic order, stripped of all evil and functioning perfectly under the watchful eye of a benevolent providence with whom the inhabitants have established a significant rapport. If the Westphalian garden is initially the unfallen world and ultimately paradise lost, then Eldorado can be viewed as Eden regained or the promised land.

Paradise in general and Eldorado in particular, where God 'a donné tout ce qu'il faut' to man is the domain of *deus fabiens* [industrious god]. The amount of work done by man in Eldorado has long been the subject of critical controversy. On the one hand, there is a palace of sciences filled with instruments of mathematics and physics, a school and government operated hotels, and on two occasions some work is actually performed: servants harness a carriage to take Candide and Cacambo to the king and three thousand engineers build a machine to hoist them out of the kingdom. On the other hand, one wonders how much work is done when there are no strangers in Eldorado and it should be remembered that Candide arrives there 'par miracle'. How much work needs to be done in the country of perfection by persons who are obviously and justifiably satisfied with their lot? Little work indeed is needed in a land where God provides everything. When compared with the other countries in the tale, it becomes apparent that Eldorado is not only the land of *deus fabiens* but of *homo otiosus* [leisure man].

It is not difficult to understand why Candide and Cacambo decide to leave Eldorado, for while they exhibit human needs, the country is not inhabited by man as we know him. When the narrator notes, therefore, that 'les deux heureux résolurent de ne plus l'être',[18] the reader wonders if the remark is serious or ironic. The text clearly indicates that in Eldorado the two vagabonds experience surprise, astonishment, curiosity, amusement and admiration. At no time is it explicitly mentioned that they are happy, or unhappy for that matter, but it is frequently indicated that they are not only strangers but of a different nature than the inhabitants. Candide is driven from the garden of Westphalia and ostensibly chooses to leave Eldorado. In the final analysis, however, he is actually driven from both gardens by the natural exigencies of his human essence. In Westphalia, he

18. The two happy men resolved to be happy no longer.

loses his innocence and acts upon his sexual urges, while in Eldorado the text suggests three reasons for his departure: woman, vanity, and restlessness. His hope of finding Cunégonde, his desire to shine among his fellows and his urge to be on the move pave the way out of the country of gold. . . .

RETURN TO THE REAL WORLD

Brilliantly couched between a chapter that deals with the cannibalistic atrocities of primitive man and one that treats the horrors of civilized man who places economic values above and beyond human dignity, the Eldorado anecdote forms the centrepiece of an ironic triptych that portrays a fleeting glance at sub-civilization, super-civilization and so-called civilization. Eldorado, the best of all possible worlds and land of the return of the golden age, is therefore in glaring opposition to the civilizations that precede and succeed it in the text. Eldorado is to the real world as being is to becoming. It is the realm of the eternal present of mythical time where change does not occur inasmuch as the tensions of history have been extirpated. It is indeed the cultivated garden and as such offers no challenge to man as we know him and, as the cultivated garden, it is truly mythical in nature because it is complete. . . .

Whereas Candide's entrance into Eldorado took the form of an ascent, his departure from the country of gold can be viewed as a descent. He is hoisted over the surrounding mountains in a fabulous machine that casts him back into the real world. His descent from the mountain ultimately evolves into a *descendus ad infernam* [descent into hell]. The dark nature of this descent is rendered doubly effective by the fact that the bright tones of Eldorado serve as its backdrop. . . .

Candide's initiatory *descendus ad infernam* is an ironic one that stands myth on its head, for the final initiatory cycle, begun in chapter nineteen and completed at the conclusion of the tale, is, in essence, the revelation of the profane. Candide's initiation is slow and painful but definitive and when viewed in the light of Eldorado appears as an evolution from stasis to dynamism. The symbolic death in this case is the death of the myth wish in the hero and the rebirth of chronological historical time, the end of the sacred and the rebirth of the profane, and, on the psychological level, the end of the childhood of our would-be *puer aeternus* [eternal youth] and the acceptance of the responsibilities of manhood.

CANDIDE'S GARDEN: CULTIVATING SOCIAL HARMONY

In the final chapter of the tale, Candide visits two more gardens and the famous dervish before founding a collective enterprise. It is only at this point, when he is finally reunited with Cunégonde, now ugly and shrewish, that he awakens from his dream of futurity and reconciles himself to the present. There is a definite progression here as we move from garden to garden. Cacambo's garden, which will be the physical *locus* of Candide's, is characterized by solitary work, while that of the Turk, who never informs himself of what is taking place in Constantinople, exists only on the familial level and eschews all social commitment. Candide's garden, on the contrary, exists at the social level, stresses positive activity, communal work, the concept of limits and human solidarity.

Unlike [scholar William] Bottiglia who argues for continuity between Eldorado and Candide's garden, I would suggest discontinuity. First of all, we have seen that Eldorado represents the cultivated garden whereas Candide's garden needs cultivation. The major thrust of *Candide* has been the refutation of Leibnizian optimism and with it the view that ours is the best of all possible worlds. At the end of the tale, not only the reader, but even Candide realizes that, at the social level, our world can be ameliorated. It is precisely the function of the final garden to demonstrate metaphorically how this can be accomplished. Whence the emerging image of *homo fabiens* which, needless to say, is radically juxtaposed with that of *homo otiosus* of the Eldorado anecdote. As regards work in the tale before the final garden, [critic] René Pomeau has admirably depicted its degrading nature. Throughout the first twenty-nine chapters of the tale, the only fluctuation in the nature of work is from exploitation to slavery. We need only think of 'le nègre de Surinam' [the negro of Surinam] and the two convicts aboard the galley—not to mention Giroflée or Paquette—to recapture the humiliation that accompanies work in the tale. In Candide's garden, however, a newly found dignity is attributed to work. This is not tantamount, nonetheless, to accepting the 'happy ending' theory of both Bottiglia and [critic] Jean Sareil, for the ending of *Candide* is just as much a beginning and there is no attainment of happiness by the protagonists. The tale ends on the *hope* of a terrestrial harvest. This harvest is only possible through work which is *ipso facto* meaningful and positive and, although neither a metaphysical nor physical panacea, is both an anodyne and a nutriment.

Whereas Eldorado was depicted as the static world of being, Candide's garden represents the dynamic world of becoming. This dynamic view of reality in the process of becoming could hardly be founded upon the perfected world of Eldorado. Indeed Candide's garden is no longer a *locus amœnus,* for man suffers here and is condemned to build a place for himself in a garden that is oblivious to his presence. . . .

On the psychological level, the last garden indicates that Candide moves to maturity and simultaneously to subjectivity, individuality and self-consciousness. This is revealed when he silences his former mentor and urges his companions to work collectively. In essence, we witness the fulfilment of the identity quest as Candide finally understands his role as a human being in history. [Swiss psychoanalyst Carl] Jung notes in this respect that '"child" means something evolving towards independence. This it cannot do without detaching itself from its origins: abandonment is therefore a necessary condition, not just a concomitant symptom'. This initiation to manhood, which is therefore both an end and a beginning, helps Candide to definitively situate himself temporally in the universe. Now in the realm of history, Candide stoically stifles the *Urzeit* [primitive times]and the *Endzeit* [end times] to courageously embrace the present.

As suggested above, Candide's garden is outside the realm of myth. Unlike the Westphalian and Eldoradean gardens which existed at the *axis mundi* and reflected the architectonic symbolism of the centre, the umbilical cord that leads to absolute reality has been cut in the final garden and the protagonists find themselves stranded in an unfathomable historical universe disassociated from mythic structures. The whole rhythm of the book has been from myth to history, from the sacred to the profane and, in an obvious myth reversal, from cosmos to chaos.

CHAPTER 3

The Artistry of the Narrative

READINGS ON
CANDIDE

Using Irony as a Form of Satire

George R. Havens

In the following excerpt, George R. Havens explores Voltaire's use of irony in his satire, pointing out specific targets and analyzing Voltaire's particular purposes. Havens also examines Voltaire's linguistic and stylistic uses of irony, exploring the artistry behind the methods by which Voltaire accomplishes his ends in *Candide*. Havens was a professor emeritus of romance languages at Ohio State University in 1934, when this work was originally published.

In sentence after sentence [Voltaire's] ready irony flashes out in potent thrusts at human foibles or wickedness or at the ridiculousness or the cruelty of human institutions. Thus, brief as it is, *Candide* is an extraordinarily complete picture of what human life is, but ought not to be. It is at once the broadest of indictments and by implication a whole program of reform.

Pride of rank appears in German insistence upon *quartiers*[1] of noble birth or the Baron's persistent refusal to consent to Candide's marriage with Cunégonde. Similarly the Governor of Buenos Ayres, Don Fernando d'Ibaraa y Figueora y Mascarenes y Lampourdos y Souza, struts his brief moment across the stage with a haughtiness befitting his wealth of sonorous names. Court flattery is deftly hit in a quick reference to laughter evoked by the jokes of the Westphalian Baron of Thunder-ten-tronckh. The dignity of the Baroness's three hundred plump pounds wins a sentence from Voltaire. Private enemies, Père Croust, Fréron, Maupertuis, the *Journal de Trévoux*, the Dutch publisher Van Düren, the Jesuits, are among those who feel the sting of his satire in allusions now obscure to the general reader but full of reality when they were written.

1. quarterings—a method of determining a person's lineage based on parents, grandparents, etc.

Excerpted from George R. Havens, *Voltaire: Candide, ou l'optimisme*, (New York: Holt, Rinehart and Winston, Inc., 1969). Reprinted with permission from the author's estate.

More important is Voltaire's attack upon human greed for gold and precious stones implied when Candide and Cacambo pick up the dust and pebbles of El Dorado. Avarice and trickery appear in the ship captain Vanderdendur (who is the Van Düren mentioned above), as he makes away with the bulk of Candide's wealth. There is the heartless ingratitude of the sailor who indifferently watches his rescuer, the Anabaptist Jacques, while the sea sweeps him overboard to death. The Protestant minister in Holland attacks the Pope instead of practicing charity. Gambling and cheating at cards feature Candide's visit to the salon of Mme de Parolignac as her victims endeavor by trickery to "réparer les cruautés du sort."[2] There are corsairs and pirates on the Mediterranean and on the high seas. No wonder that at the spectacle of so much wickedness Candide bursts out: "Croyez-vous . . . que les hommes se soient toujours mutuellement massacrés, comme ils font aujourd'hui, qu'ils aient toujours été menteurs, fourbes, perfides, ingrats, brigands, faibles, volages, lâches, envieux, gourmands, ivrognes, avares, ambitieux, sanguinaires, calomniateurs, débauchés, fanatiques, hypocrites et sots?"[3]

SATIRIZING SOCIAL INSTITUTIONS

But Voltaire does not limit himself to attacking individual human foibles or wickedness. More dangerous still are the manifestations of ferocity or cruelty in what have become established institutions of society. Judges and courts are as indifferent to justice in Surinam as in England or Paris. Worst of all no doubt is that murder on a large scale which is called war. The Bulgars and the Abars typify the Prussians and the French then in the midst of the Seven Years' War. All the "heroic butchery" of battle, the burning, pillaging, and ravishing of men amuck with primeval savagery, are sketched by Voltaire in a few swift sentences which are only the more effective because of their skillful brevity. Military drill and discipline witnessed from the palace windows of Potsdam receive their due share of the author's cutting irony. Among the anomalies which constantly called forth Voltaire's scorn was the spectacle of the Church blessing

2. repair the cruel blows of fate 3. Do you think that men have always massacred each other the way they do now? That they've always been liars, cheats, traitors, ingrates, brigands? That they've always been fickle, feeble, envious, gluttonous, drunken, avaricious, ambitious, bloodthirsty, slanderous, debauched, fanatical, hypocritical, and stupid?

war. On both sides of the lines *Te Deum* was being said, thanksgiving for victory or prayer to ward off defeat. Christianity, which professed human brotherhood, accepted and supported war, the negation of all its moral and ethical

---

EARLY CRITICISM AND RESPONSE

These two pieces complement each other well and provide an interesting reaction to Candide *from authors who were alive much closer to Voltaire's time than readers today are; these reactions are more immediate, without the benefit of years of discussion and analysis concerning the book. Both are taken from* Voltaire's "Candide" and the Critics, *edited by Milton P. Foster.*

"This Dull Product of a Scoffer's Pen"
William Wordsworth

The book, which in my hand
Had opened of itself (for it was swoln
With searching damp, and seemingly had lain
To the injurious elements exposed
From week to week,) I found to be a work
In the French tongue, a Novel of Voltaire,
        His famous Optimist.

. . . . .

. . . this dull product of a scoffer's pen,
Impure conceits discharging from a heart
Hardened by impious pride!

"A Masterpiece of Wit"
William Hazlitt

Candide is a masterpiece of wit. It has been called 'the dull product of a scoffer's pen'; it is indeed the 'product of a scoffer's pen'; but after reading the Excursion, few people will think it *dull.* It is in the most perfect keeping, and without any appearance of effort. Every sentence tells, and the whole reads like one sentence. There is something sublime in Martin's sceptical indifference to moral good and evil. It is the repose of the grave. It is better to suffer this living death, than a living martyrdom. 'Nothing can touch him further.' The moral of *Candide* (such as it is) is the same as that of *Rasselas:* the execution is different. Voltaire says, 'A great book is a great evil.' Dr. [Samuel] Johnson would have laboured this short apophthegm into a voluminous common-place.

Milton P. Foster, ed., *Voltaire's* Candide *and the Critics,* Belmont, CA: Wadsworth, 1962.

ideals. So-called Christian nations actually furnished arms to the Moors against other Christians. There is irony in the fact that a Jesuit officer could be at the same time Colonel and Priest. International law legalizes the violation of human rights. The Church itself has its Inquisition and burns heretics in a so-called Act of Faith, Auto-da-fé, while ladies witness the ceremony and eat refreshments. Christians are held in slavery by the Moors. The former in turn practice negro slavery and treat their slaves with a cruelty which no civilization should countenance. The Jesuits in Paraguay rule with complete indifference to the rights and welfare of their native subjects. Galley slaves toil over their oars beneath the lash of their cruel overseers.

Human beliefs, social classes, music, art and literature, France, Germany, Italy, Spain, Portugal, America, Turkey, the scourges of disease and catastrophe, all are the objects of satire from Voltaire's pen. The picture is complete, too complete even for enumeration in brief space. Any careful reader of *Candide* could fill in numerous details here omitted.

At first sight so black a picture may seem the work of a confirmed pessimist who looks upon humanity with despairing eyes. Not so, however. Of course, *Candide* is intentionally one-sided. No carefully balanced account of good and evil could shock mankind into revolt. Only the unremitting hammering of Voltaire's attack could penetrate the armor of complacency and indifference with which humanity is but too well fortified. Stupid indeed and smug must he be, however, who can read *Candide* without something of the moral jolt intended by its author. Once shaken from acceptance of long existing evils, humanity may then proceed to "cultivate its garden." Voltaire has pointed out the weeds. There is work to be done. Let every one bear a hand. This is the counsel of *Candide*, not a counsel of despair, of pessimism, and defeat. It is a counsel of courage, of work, of accomplishment, in the face of clear-seeing recognition of human wickedness and misery. Voltaire's philosophy is eminently practical.

VOLTAIRE'S STYLE AND IRONIC METHOD

Against the abuses just mentioned Voltaire employs that most potent weapon of ridicule. Men fear nothing so much as to be laughed at. But what are some of the stylistic methods by which his effects are obtained? Without attempting a detailed analysis of Voltaire's art as a writer, it is worth while to indicate a few typical characteristics of his style in *Candide*, that masterpiece of its kind in the world's literature.

One device commonly employed is that of intentional understatement. Instead of hyperbole and exaggeration—which are likewise used with telling effect—Voltaire frequently states mildly what is obviously most grave. The reader, who perceives the discrepancy, is but the more impressed. For example, Candide's partial recovery from the beating in the Bulgarian army is indicated by the simple phrase: "Il avait déjà *un peu* de peau et *pouvait marcher.*" [4] The evils of the Old World are commented upon by Candide as he sails toward the New: "Il faut avouer qu'on pourrait gémir *un peu* de ce qui se passe dans le nôtre en physique et en morale." [5] Pangloss and Candide "furent menés séparément dans des appartements d'une extrême fraîcheur, dans lesquels on n'était jamais incommodé du soleil." [6] Closely allied to this method is Voltaire's frequent stating of the most atrocious abuses or absurdities with an affected indifference as though they were the most natural and commonplace things in the world, as indeed they all too often are. Thus: "Il était décidé par l'Université de Coïmbre que le spectacle de quelques personnes brûlées à petit feu en grande cérémonie est un secret infaillible pour empêcher la terre de trembler." [7] On the return from South America, the travelers came upon a combat at sea between a Spanish ship and a Dutch pirate. The wind brought the two vessels so near "qu'on eut *le plaisir* de voir le combat *tout à son aise.*" [8] The same indifferent simplicity heightens the effect of the account given of the horrible treatment of negro slaves. "Quand nous travaillons aux sucreries et que la meule nous attrape le doigt, on nous coupe la main; quand nous voulons nous enfuir, on nous coupe la jambe; je me suis trouvé dans les deux cas." [9]

The grammatically logical union of illogical absurdities is another favorite device. The Baron was one of the most powerful lords of Westphalia, "*car* son château avait une porte et des fenêtres." [10] One recalls the classical example: "Les nez ont été faits pour porter des lunettes, *aussi* avons-nous des

4. He already had *a little* skin and *could walk.* 5. You have to admit, one could grumble rather at what goes on in ours, both physically and morally. 6. were led away to separate apartments, which were extremely cool and where the sun was never troublesome 7. It was decided by the University of Coimbra that the spectacle of a few people being ceremoniously burnt over a low flame is the infallible secret of preventing earthquakes. 8. that they had *the pleasure* of seeing the engagement *in perfect comfort* 9. When we're working at the sugar-mill and catch our finger in the grinding-wheel, they cut off our hand. When we try to run away, they cut off a leg. I have been in both these situations. 10. *for* his castle had a door and windows

lunettes. Les jambes sont visiblement instituées pour être chaussées, *et* nous avons des chausses."[11] Maître Pangloss is described as "le plus grand philosophe de la province, et *par conséquent* de toute la terre."[12]

Sharp and unexpected contrast is effectively employed. The Bulgarian soldiers congratulated Candide: "'Votre fortune est faite, et votre gloire est assurée.' On lui met sur-lechamp les fers aux pieds, et on le mène au régiment."[13] There Candide, given only ten blows on the third day of military drill, "est regardé par ses camarades comme un prodige."[14] In commenting upon the battle, great effect is obtained by the mere juxtaposition of the two words "boucherie héroïque" [heroic butchery].

Similar is the working up to an unexpected conclusion. The host of the inn on the confines of El Dorado tells Candide and Cacambo: "Je suis fort ignorant, *et je m'en trouve bien.*"[15] The two travelers "entrèrent dans une maison fort simple, *car* la porte n'était que *d'argent*, et les lambris des appartements n'étaient que d'*or*."[16] The government of the Jesuits in Paraguay is remarkable: "Los Padres y ont tout, et les peuples rien; c'est *le chef-d'œuvre de la raison et de la nature.*"[17] Candide, fleeing from Buenos Ayres, bemoans his separation from Cunégonde: "A quoi me servira de prolonger mes misérables jours, puisque je dois les traîner loin d'elle dans les remords et dans le désespoir? et que dira *le Journal de Trévoux?*"[18] The King of the Bulgars (a reminiscence of Frederick the Great) pardoned Candide "avec une clémence qui sera louée dans tous les journaux et *dans tous les siècles.*"[19] Perhaps the best example of all is the account of the battle between the Bulgars and the Abars. "Rien n'était si beau, si leste, si brillant, si bien ordonné que les deux armées. Les trompettes, les fifres, les hautbois, les tambours, les canons formaient une *harmonie telle qu'il n'y en eut jamais en enfer.*"[20] Nothing forecasts the magnificent anticli-

11. Noses were made to bear spectacles, *and so* we have spectacles. Legs are evidently devised to be clad in breeches, *and* breeches we have. 12. the greatest philospher in the province and *therefore* in the whole world 13. Your fortune is made and your glory assured. His feet were promptly clapped in irons and he was taken off to the regiment. 14. his comrades thought him a prodigy 15. I know very little about things, and that suits me well enough. 16. entered a house of a very modest sort, for its front door was only of silver and the panelling of its room merely gold 17. Los Padres own everything in it, and the people nothing—a masterpiece of reason and justice. 18. What's the use of prolonging my miserable existence if I must drag it out, far away from her, in remorse and despair? And what will the *Journal de Trévoux* say? 19. with a clemency that will be praised in every newspaper and *in every century* 20. Never was there anything so fine, so dashing, so glittering, or so well-regulated as those two armies. The trumpets, the fifes, the hautboys, the drums, and the cannon produced a *harmony such as never was heard in hell.*

max of the last phrase until it suddenly appears before the eyes of the reader.

In contrast to the method of understatement mentioned at the beginning is the use of superlatives with intentional exaggeration. "Le plus beau des châteaux," la belle Cunégonde," "le meilleur des mondes," "le plus grand métaphysicien,"[21] etc., furnish examples at once apparent to the reader. These and other similar phrases gain in effect by the intentional repetition with which they are hammered in. This repetition is in fact one more of the stylistic devices used by Voltaire throughout *Candide*.

There are happy *trouvailles* like: "Nous ferons bonne chère; mangeons du jésuite, mangeons du jésuite,"[22] as one might say: "mangeons du jambon."[23] Having failed to kill the Baron in their previous combat, Candide menaces him with: "Je te *re*tuerais."[24] The gold and jewels of El Dorado are reduced to what they are, except for conventional associations, yellow sand and pretty pebbles. Thus effective statement takes the place of lengthy argument.

Finally one must mention of course the use of short, crisp sentences, the simplicity of the purely narrative passages, the elimination of all connectives except the bare minimum, as Lanson says, so that the sentences gallop and race along at top speed. These are some of the well-known characteristics of Voltaire's style in *Candide* which, with the others that have been pointed out, give it an excellence and a quality all its own and make it the despair of every imitator.

21. The most beautiful of castles, the beautiful Cunegonde, the greatest philosopher 22. Our stomachs will be full. Let's eat Jesuit! Let's eat Jesuit 23. let's eat ham. 24. I'll *re*-kill you.

Using Low Comedy to Mock Philosophic Pretensions

Clifton Cherpak

Clifton Cherpak looks at *Candide*'s relationship to the romance, the burlesque, the satire, and the philosophical tale, and he concludes that while the novel is technically excellent, it may disappoint those who are looking for a grandiose statement against intolerance and injustice. In Cherpak's view, Voltaire uses aspects of low comedy to poke fun at those who seek grand philosophical theories to explain human affairs. This essay originally appeared in *Approaches to Teaching Voltaire's "Candide."*

Candide's academic popularity, that students read it from junior high school through graduate school and in many different kinds of courses, encourages one to forget that it is primarily a literary work, a kind of fiction. The expert giving an advanced undergraduate course is often tempted to regard this philosophical tale as the epitome of Voltairean thought. Many teachers of survey courses in French civilization and culture find it only too convenient as a compressed representation of the spirit of the Enlightenment. In a survey course in French literature, *Candide* lends itself only too easily to thematic discussion. These approaches are not, of course, completely wrongheaded, but they do tend to obscure the work's fundamentally literary nature, its technical merits, and, not least, its basic joke.

From a literary standpoint, *Candide* is a parody, or, more precisely, a burlesque, since it mimics on a ridiculously low level a much more exalted kind of work. In fact, it is a double burlesque. Candide's expulsion from the château of the Baron de Thunder-ten-tronckh and his adventurous wanderings until he winds up at the farm near the Propontide

Excerpted from Clifton Cherpak, *"Candide* as a Literary Form," in *Approaches to Teaching Voltaire's "Candide,"* edited by Renee Waldinger. Copyright © 1987 The Modern Language Association of America. Reprinted with permission from The Modern Language Association of America.

are certainly intended to invoke the great biblical Fall and the postlapsarian wanderings of tribes of Israel until they reach the Promised Land. Within this frame, the narrative also burlesques an ancient and durable form of Western prose fiction: the romance.

ELEMENTS OF THE ROMANCE

In the archetypal romance (what classical scholars call the Greek "erotic" romance), an unusually handsome boy meets an unusually beautiful girl; they fall in love; they are separated by forces beyond their control; they traverse a series of lands and seas; they experience adventures, the return of characters believed lost, interpolated stories, recapitulations, and excursuses until they are reunited; and, after succeeding in various trials of the boy's valor and the girl's virginity, they are wed.

As developed by such writers as Achilles Tatius and Heliodorus, and as imitated in countless novels familiar to the readers of Voltaire's time, the romance is, although long and seemingly heavy with privations and dangerous adventures, a buoyant, optimistic genre, celebrating human energy and persistence before its terminal heralding of the formation of a new, vigorous, sane society. Voltaire humorously inverts typical features of the romance, perhaps recalling for his first readers the earliest known subversion of the romance form, Petronius's *Satyricon.* The basic joke of that Roman novel is that both lovers are rascals, and both are male. Today's undergraduate readers will probably know none of these early works, and, since the truly typical romances are too long to assign for background reading, students have to rely for their appreciation of the burlesque on the instructor's powers of description (powers, incidentally, that should be enriched by a reading of Heliodorus's *Aethiopica,* a seminal text if there ever was one).

ELEMENTS OF THE BURLESQUE

The burlesque elements of *Candide* are important for appreciation of *Candide*'s humor, but the contrasts between Voltaire's parody and the norms of the original—especially at the end, where the weary, disabused, and dilapidated characters scarcely promise a vital and virtuous new society—are more than merely funny in an ironic way. *Candide* is a fundamentally serious work: a satire.

In his *Anatomy of Criticism,* Northrop Frye assigns *Candide* to the second of six phases of satire. In this phase, "The satirist demonstrates the infinite variety of what men do by showing the futility, not only of saying what they ought to do, but even of attempts to systematize or formulate a coherent scheme of what they do." The central strategy of this phase consists in "setting of ideas and generalizations over against the life they are supposed to explain."

This idea helps us focus on the basic message in *Candide,* emphasizing the story rather than the ideas in the work. The point is not that certain ideas are wrong or foolishly conceived but that they are basically irrelevant to living. In other words, philosophical systems may be elegant, may even be irrefutable on logical grounds, but they are still irrelevant in a practical sense, because people are incapable, by and large, of living according to systems of any kind.

For example, in his first literary attack on Leibnizian optimism, the *Poem on the Disaster in Lisbon,* Voltaire does not criticize the inability of Leibniz's philosophical system to account for the evil represented by the earthquake and tidal wave that destroyed Lisbon and many of its inhabitants. What he decries is that Leibniz leaves no room for lamentation. Too neat, too comprehensive, and thus too inhuman, Leibniz's system is inadequate not as explanation but as consolation.

Candide itself demonstrates that this system is irrelevant to the basic human needs, hopes, fears, and dreams so insistently presented in the story. Thematically, Voltaire shows how lust and vanity have more control over human behavior than do philosophical ideas. Stylistically, he consistently uses the non sequitur, not to criticize the technical inadequacy of Leibnizian optimism, but to show the contrast between theory and practice, or between expectation and event. Early in the work, Voltaire's use of the word *car* ("for") sets the pattern. The first chapter explains that the baron was one of the most important noblemen in Westphalia, "for his house had a door and several windows" (all translations mine), and that Candide believed innocently in Pangloss's philosophical teachings, "for he found mademoiselle Cunégonde extremely beautiful." A frequent variation on this non sequitur in reasoning is what might be called the circumstantial non sequitur: the recruiters for the Bulgarian army in chapter 2 congratulate Candide and immediately put him in irons, the women being chased by the monkeys burst into tears when Candide kills them, Candide's illness becomes serious because of the administration of medicines, and so on.

Most of the non sequiturs in *Candide* do not refer explicitly to Leibniz's philosophy, since Voltaire wants us to see that the world in general is absurd, but some function more explicitly as philosophical satire. In the fourth chapter, Pangloss explains that since private misfortunes contribute to the general good, more of the one causes more of the other, and that if Columbus had not caught syphilis in the New World Europeans would not have chocolate or cochineal. Here Voltaire mocks, of course, Leibniz's use of cause-and-effect reasoning to reinforce his theory of necessity. The irrelevance of such reasoning, even when cleverly and convincingly executed, is best exemplified in the last paragraph of the tale. There, Pangloss explains that if Candide had not had the sequence of experiences that followed his expulsion from the Baron's château he would not be where he is, eating candied fruit and pistachio nuts. Candide acknowledges both the truth and the irrelevance of this chain of reasoning by saying: "That is well said, but we must cultivate our garden."

ANIMAL APPETITES

When asked why philosophy and reason are not the guides of the characters in *Candide*, my own students usually point out, with varying degrees of satisfaction, that they are mostly sex maniacs. On that basis alone, students are willing to accept the notion that *Candide* is less a satire of philosophy than a satire of human behavior, frequently showing us that people are much closer to the beasts than to the gods: the monkeys killed by Candide represent a level of "love" no lower than that of most of the human characters. At the end of chapter 21, this point is made more explicitly. When asked whether human beings have always been as base and disgusting as they seem to Candide, Martin asks in turn if hawks have always eaten pigeons. When Candide is desperate to leave France at the end of chapter 22, he says that he has seen monkeys worrying tigers, and bears in his own castle, but has seen men only in Eldorado. To make the association even clearer, the "dervish" at the end of the tale, when asked why such a strange animal as the human being was made and why suffering abounds, compares God to a king, the world to a ship, and human beings to mice in the hold.

References to food throughout the tale also reinforce the theme of our insistent animal appetites. In chapter 7, after a description of Candide's unmerciful flogging, the text says: "In spite of his misfortunes, Candide ate and slept." In chapter 16, after Candide wonders why he should continue his miserable existence, there is a characteristic and telling sentence: "While giving vent to these melancholy reflections, Candide was eating a hearty meal." Indeed, even adherence to philosophical views is conditioned by hunger and its satisfaction. In a passage near the beginning of chapter 20, we find: "when he spoke of Cunégonde, especially at the end of a meal, he leaned towards Pangloss's system."

The quality exemplified here, which also makes the old woman say at the end of chapter 12 that, although she has wanted to kill herself a hundred times, she is still in love with life, has nothing specific to do with the Enlightenment. It is, quite simply, the power of the life force, which, through the operation of appetites, drives us on, sometimes to trouble and suffering, but which, unlike the charms of art and culture in the Pococurante episode, almost never flags. In this regard, Voltaire, although in an ironic register, is true to the genre he burlesques, for the romance, with its proliferation of episodes, its repeated reboundings and recommencements, provides an excellent vehicle for a demonstration of the life force in action, even when youth, beauty, and the promise of a brave new world are gone.

CANDIDE'S TECHNICAL EXCELLENCE

In fact, the congruity between form and motifs and between motifs and norms constitutes the technical excellence of *Candide* and its superiority to Voltaire's other philosophical tales. The best way to help students appreciate this superiority is to have them read [Voltaire's earlier works] *Zadig* and *L'ingénu* along with *Candide*, especially in the light of the first phase of satire as described by Northrop Frye. In this phase, that of the low norm, the absurd and corrupt society is left intact, and the message to the reader is that one must either keep a very low profile or at least appear to accept the conventions of society if one is to survive.

Both *Zadig* and *L'ingénu* are formal hybrids, and both juxtapose satirical norms. *Zadig* starts out as a sequence of typical oriental anecdotes and then turns into a typical romance. Zadig, usually characterized by intelligence and initiative, is passive in the episode of the Angel, which sets a high norm. He remembers this norm for the rest of his life, but he also keeps in mind the brigand and the grain of sand that turns into a diamond, which represent a much lower norm. *L'ingénu* begins as a typical form of satire in which an outsider, by his naiveté, uncovers the absurdity and corruption of civilization, but it turns into a kind of fiction known in France as an *histoire tragique*. Once again norms are juxtaposed in a way that renders interpretation impossible, for the Huron hero, whose noble innocence served to point up the evils of society, abandons his pride and his nobility, embraces civilization, and becomes its servant.

Given the consistency of form and the coherence of motifs in *Candide*, students might expect that the interpretation of this, Voltaire's most perfect, most popular tale, would be comparatively simple. However, teachers should inform them that "experts" have seriously, even passionately, advanced just about every conceivable interpretation of Voltaire's final injunction concerning the cultivation of one's garden. The obvious advantage of this revelation is that students will feel free to try their own interpretive wings. In addition, awareness of this continuing disagreement may teach students a lesson about expertise that Voltaire would have applauded.

THE LOW NORM

Of course, instructors can explain that, according to deconstructionism, determinate meaning is a quaint bourgeois myth and that every decoding is a new encoding. If that possibility seems undesirable, they can legitimately point out that literary form is a shaper rather than a container and that it limits, therefore, the range of relevant interpretation. In the case of *Candide*, the retirement of the characters at the end and the accepted lesson of the old man—who ignores Constantinople and has found that work banishes the three great evils: boredom, vice, and poverty—makes it clear that Candide ends on a low norm. Consequently, the final message concerning the cultivation of one's garden is probably not symbolic or allegorical, such as a call to arms in the fight against the ancien régime or organized religion, as has been claimed. My own view is that Voltaire simply suggests that keeping quietly busy is the safest and most satisfactory way to live in an absurd and dangerous world.

This interpretation, although congenial, one might suppose, to future accountants and tax lawyers, may well disappoint instructors who want to introduce Voltaire in class as the premier fighter against intolerance and injustice, the prince of the philosophes, and the star of the French Enlightenment. He was those things, by and large, but his philosophical tales, most of which present a low norm regardless of Voltaire's attitudes at the moments of composition, are not the best vehicles for such an introduction. This dominance of the low norm is puzzling, but much that concerns the Voltairean philosophical tale is puzzling, including the purpose and the public that Voltaire had in mind for them. These enigmas, of course, have kept scholars busy, thereby helping them to avoid boredom, vice, and need. *Candide*, it would seem, not only continues to be popular but also has clearly become functional, at least for its professional readers.

Finally, it might also be pointed out that Voltaire, who considered himself above all a man of letters and who expected to be remembered as the foremost tragedian of his age, took a dim view of prose fiction in general. Indicative of his distaste for this low form of literature was his habit of applying the generic term *novel* to works that he detested. It is, indeed, ironic that he has been for some time best known (and, to many, only known) as the author of *Candide*. But since he played so many jokes on the world, it may be some kind of justice that the world, through the persistent popularity of this small work and the comparative eclipse of his weightier texts, has played a joke on him.

Voltaire's Black Humor

Alan R. Pratt

Alan R. Pratt, an associate professor of Humanities at Embry-Riddle Aeronautical University in Florida, examines Voltaire's use of black humor and shows his influence on the works of contemporary authors. Pratt argues that *Candide* has had a great effect on modern writers who confront mankind's inhumanity to fellow human beings by presenting the human condition absurdly, ironically, and humorously. In doing so, Voltaire and the contemporary authors condemn such "wretchedness" by presenting evil in the world as something to mock and hold in disdain.

Andre Breton named Jonathan Swift the originator of black humor, but few critics have examined the relationship between contemporary works of black humor and "A Modest Proposal" or *Gulliver's Travels*. Instead, essays about black humor which include the past often refer to Voltaire's *Candide*, and one can find it referenced in discussions of works by Céline, Heller, Barth, Pynchon, Vonnegut and Southern, to name but a few. *Candide* is quite different from Voltaire's other philosophical tales because though the work focuses on metaphysical concerns, rather than social or psychological matters, it ends with a pessimistic assessment of the human condition. It seems clear that Voltaire was wrestling with the same philosophical/existential quandaries that are addressed in the twentieth century literature of the absurd. And that black humorists have been influenced by *Candide* is not surprising because Voltaire worked with a combination of elements which have come to be identified with the modern black humor novel.

SIMILARITIES BETWEEN SATIRE AND BLACK HUMOR

Candide has generally been identified as traditional satire attacking a variety of subjects but focusing on [scientist Gott-

fried] Leibniz's notion of " pre-established harmony." To attack what he perceived as absurd, Voltaire used absurdity,
relying on the tools, character types and stylistic flourishes
that constitute traditional satiric strategies. But to categorize
Candide as satire overlooks the fact that while Voltaire's
comic invective is value destructive, it is not ameliorative.
And modern literary black humor is differentiated from
satire for precisely this reason—it relies on the tools of satirical prose to create an apocalyptic reality, but it neither attempts to distinguish between the ideal and reality nor ad-
vocates an alternative ordering.

The plot of *Candide* is simple: Candide loses his love
Cunegonde, and in search of her he travels around the
world. On much of the journey, he is accompanied by the
unflappable Dr. Pangloss who can demonstrate, *reductio ad
obsurdum*, that "things cannot be otherwise. . . . noses were
made to wear spectacles. . . . Legs were clearly devised for
breeches. . . ." The doctor's best-of-all-possible-worlds view
is entirely convincing to Candide who admires Pangloss,
seeing him as one of the world's most profound savants.

Critics have commented on the obvious similarities of
Candide's relationship with Pangloss and the relationship
between Ebenezer Cook, the naive protagonist of John
Barth's *The Sot-Weed Factor*, and his teacher, Henry
Burlingame. That Barth might emulate features of *Candide*
is not surprising. In a number of contexts, Barth has explained that he creates something new by using something
old, of using exhausted forms in new ways. In his later novels, this manifests itself as a genius for parody. Not just
Barth, though, employs parody; other black humorists have
also recognized its liberating possibilities. Terry Southern, to
cite one example, created an elaborate parody with *Candy*, a
risqué version of Voltaire's masterpiece. Parody is, in fact, a
favorite strategy of black humorists as it undermines the authority of the parodied genre. Although the literary pedigree
of *Candide* can be traced to the picaresque (also a favorite
form of black humorists), Voltaire burlesqued the literature
of his day as his tale parodies the eighteenth century romance with its precocious "hero gallant" and distressed
damsel.

That *Candide* and the modern black humor novel share a
similar comic technique is not much in itself. But there are
other similarities. Voltaire's *conte*, for instance, begins with a

mock-historic title page: "translated from the German of doctor Ralph with additions which were found in the Doctor's pocket when he died at Minden in the Year of Our Lord 1759." In his later novels Barth distracts readers with similar tricks in addition to creating complex pseudo-histories. Raymond Olderman calls attention to the same ploy adopted by many other black humorists to add "authenticity," blurring the line between reality and fantasy.

In addition to the outright fabrication of histories, the black humor novel frequently weaves actual events, albeit exaggerated, into the narrative. Bruce Jay Friedman said that *The New York Times* was "the source and fountain and bible of black humor." And Barth's *Sot-Weed Factor* and Tom Berger's *Little Big Man*, to name just two, depend on a loose interpretation of actual events. Voltaire does precisely the same thing. The Lisbon earthquake, the Jesuit dictatorship of Peru, slavery in Surinam, the execution of Admiral John Byng, the inquisition, and the Seven Years War between Prussia and the French alliance were all very real catastrophes, though filtered through the artist's mind and transformed in his art.

The Seven Years War, for instance, is used as a setting in an early episode. Shortly after Candide begins his sojourn, he is shanghaied by two recruiters and forced into the war. The battlefield then becomes a source of macabre humor: "First the cannons laid low about six thousand men on each side, then rifle fire removed from the best of worlds about nine or ten thousand scoundrels who had been infesting its surface." This sardonic description is followed by scenes which occasion not laughter but revulsion:

> Old men with wounds all over their bodies were watching the death throes of butchered women who clutched their children to their bloody breasts; girls who had been disemboweled after satisfying the natural needs of several heroes were breathing their last sighs; others, mortally burned, were shrieking for someone to hasten their death; the ground was strewn with brains and severed arms and legs.

By juxtaposing—or integrating—comic understatement with gut-wrenching realism, Voltaire anticipates the same strategy cultivated and refined by the black humorists. In *Journey to the End of Night*, for example, Louis-Ferdinand Céline initiates Bardamu's misadventures with the experience of war. Thomas Pynchon uses a fantasy of war as an image of death in *Gravity's Rainbow*. In *Slaughterhouse Five*

Kurt Vonnegut flippantly references the fire-bombing of Dresden where "135,000 Hansels and Gretels . . . baked like gingerbread men." And in *Catch-22* Joseph Heller regularly connects comical moments with combat horrors.

JUXTAPOSITIONS

Throughout *Candide*, Voltaire juxtaposes the comic and the tragic. Likewise, contemporary uses of the technique are not limited to the context of war, but are found in every conceivable circumstance—startling juxtapositions between subjects or between subject and form is, in fact, the hallmark of black humor. And in the rapidly progressing episodes of *Candide*, Voltaire finds opportunity to lampoon the human condition using many of the topics that are regularly identified with modern black humor, including social, religious and philosophical systems, natural as well as man-made disasters, senseless violence, pestilence, death, mutilation, and even sexually transmitted disease.

After escaping from war, Candide finds himself in Holland where he is fortuitously reunited with the now syphilitic Dr. Pangloss who is toothless, almost blind, and whose nose and ear have been eaten away. Does syphilis come from the devil, then? No, explains Pangloss; rather, "it was an indispensable element in the best of worlds, a necessary ingredient" without which Europeans would not have chocolate. Pangloss' preposterous rationalization allows him to come to terms with the senselessness of human suffering and the inscrutable relationship between cause and effect. Two centuries later, the consequences of sexual activity will once again spark a similar line of questioning when characters from *Catch-22* are faced with the same absurd ordering of events. But rather than Pangloss' cheerful acceptance of *non sequiturs*, they are bewildered:

> There just doesn't seem to be any logic to this system of rewards and punishment. Look what happened to me. If I had gotten syphilis or a dose of clap for my five minutes of passion on the beach instead of this damned mosquito bite, I could see some justice. But malaria? *Malaria?* Who can explain malaria as a consequence of fornication? . . . just for once I'd like to see all these things sort of straightened out, with each person getting exactly what he deserves. It might give me some confidence in this universe.

While Voltaire's Pangloss links events illogically, in Heller's dark comedy, characters contemplate illogical events. In both examples, though, the message is the same: human beings are helpless when confronting an absurd reality.

RELATIVISM

The terrors which Candide and Pangloss face continue to grow in intensity; both are whipped, tortured, robbed, beaten and forced into slavery—and for the reader, the laughter seldom abates. At one point Candide is miraculously reunited with Cunegonde. Given its episodic structure, *Candide* contains many inconceivable events (like Candide's meeting with Pangloss above). These preposterous coincidences serve as transitions between episodes, but more importantly the chance escapes, separations, and meetings emphasize Voltaire's impression that contingency, not necessity, orders events. It is an impression that is similarly amplified in the literature of modern black humor.

Cosmic contingency and the relativity of experience are further underscored in *Candide* with the harrowing tale of the old woman. The crippled hag was once the beautiful, virginal daughter of a pope, destined to marry a handsome prince and live happily ever after. But for nothing more than bad luck, the woman's ship is attacked in route to her wedding, and she is repeatedly violated by the pirate crew. Later, she is rescued from a pile of bleeding corpses by a eunuch who admires her voluptuous body (and bemoans the loss of his testicles) only to be sold into slavery where she will lose one of her appetizing buttocks, and the balance of her life will be exhausted through years of abominable slavery. While the old woman's story is a litany of human barbarity, Voltaire weaves a kind of ludicrous eroticism through it. This synthesis of prurient sensuality and savage violence resembles the disturbing incongruencies which are a characteristic of contemporary black humor.

Many times the old woman has wanted to kill herself, and with her extensive experience she has ascertained that vast numbers of people also loathe their lives, though few choose suicide.

> I've wanted to kill myself a hundred times, but I still love life. That ridiculous weakness is perhaps one of our most pernicious inclinations. What could be more stupid than to persist in carrying a burden that we constantly want to cast off, to hold our existence in horror, yet cling to it nonetheless, to fondle the serpent that devours us, until it has eaten our heart.

Black humorists treat the issue of self-destruction in a senseless world with typical impertinence. In Barth's *Floating Opera*, for instance, Todd Andrews concludes, *"There's no final reason for living (or for suicide)."* After further reflection, he adds:

> To realize that nothing makes any final difference is overwhelming; but if one goes not farther and becomes a saint, a cynic, or a suicide on principle, one hasn't reasoned completely.

In contrast to Todd Andrews' rationalized apathy, Voltaire's old woman is unconcerned with the philosophical issue of suicide in an absurd world. Instead, she would like to annihilate herself, but is prohibited from self-destruction by a mysterious force which is beyond her ability to control.

Voltaire returns to the theme of relativism and moral anarchy in the Oreillon episode. Lost in a South American jungle, Candide sees two naked, screaming women being chased by monkeys. To save them, he shoots the offensive beasts only to discover that the dead animals were the women's lovers. In this instance Voltaire couples sexual activity with the grotesque to accentuate another failed attempt to impose order on a mysterious and multi-faceted reality. What is abhorrent in one context is proper pleasure in another. Black humorists are fond of illustrating similar situations, and critics have called attention to the chaotic plurality that figures prominently in the contemporary black humor. Max Schulz refers to the phenomenon as the "metaphysics of multiplicity," and considers it a principal feature of the black humor novel. Within this frame of reference, "all versions of reality are mental constructs. . . . No one is aprioristically truer than another."

At the end of Candide's and his companions' adventures, the survivors find themselves on an alien shore, exhausted and annoyed by the outcome of events: Candide has discovered that even love is an illusion. The pessimist Martin is more convinced than ever that "people are equally wretched everywhere." Cacambo, working to support the whole group, is "worn out by his work" and curses his fate. Cunegonde is "growing uglier everyday." The old woman is infirm, and even the imperturbable Pangloss despairs because he cannot "shine in some German university." Underlying their irritation is a growing sense of boredom, causing the old woman to reflect,

> I'd like to know which is worse: to be raped a hundred times
> by Negro pirates, to have one buttock cut off, to run the gaunt-
> let in the Bulgar army, to be whipped and hanged in an auto-
> da-fé, to be dissected, to be a galley slave—in short, to suffer
> all the miseries we've all gone through—or to stay here doing
> nothing.

Martin voices similar thoughts, concluding that mankind is
"born to live in either the convulsions of anxiety or the
lethargy of boredom."

THE BOREDOM OF EXISTENCE

The problem of boredom is another recurring theme in *Candide*. Even in Eldorado, where there is happiness, peace and
plenty, the novelty of perfection quickly fades, replaced by a
gnawing sense of insignificance and futility. To alleviate
their existential malaise, Candide's group consults the most
astute philosopher in Asia Minor. The dervish's response
echoes the experience of the biblical Job: "Is it any of your
business?" The best one can do, he tells them, is "Keep
quiet." This is not Voltaire's last word on meaninglessness,
however.

"Let's work without theorizing," Martin says, "it's the only
way to make life bearable." And in the end we see Candide
intently cultivating his garden, an automaton immersed in
mind-numbing labor. "In effect," Robert Adams writes, "the
machine of the world has succeeded in grinding down the
characters till they too are nothing but mechanisms." Black
humorists feel comfortable with the perception that the
pressures of a disintegrating world reduce human beings to
the functional. In *V*, for example, Pynchon's characters discover that life can be tolerable only when they learn to emulate the indifference of a machine. And Slothrop's chaotic
misadventures in *Gravity's Rainbow*, in many ways compa-
rable to Candide's, end in a kind of defensive resignation.

Without oversimplifying, it's fair to say that *Candide* resembles its distant modern progeny in a number of ways. To
depict an absurd world, Voltaire incorporated the subjects
and utilized the devices that modern black humorists have
embraced to evoke tenebrous laughter. And like the black
humor novel, Voltaire's comic masterpiece features a picaresque antihero buffeted by events which conspicuously
accent frightful and lurid realities. By the conclusion of the
conte, Voltaire has stripped the world of mollifying illusions,

offered nothing to replace them, and leaves readers with a vision of the world as a grim place governed by senseless cosmic forces. It is an outlook which is surprisingly similar to those found in books of contemporary black humorists. Where Voltaire's masterpiece differs from its modern counterparts, however, is in the conclusion.

In *Candide* the human situation is a black affair where the best one can do is adopt a kind of stoic resignation. Although the human situation is also bleak in the black humor novel, it most often endeavors "to face the void without flinching," as Ronald Wallace maintains, "to endure the absurd, and by viewing life from a comic perspective, to enjoy the endurance." The contrast between Voltaire's response to cosmic absurdity and that of modern black humorists is underscored by comparing the final scenes of *Candide* with those of Kurt Vonnegut's *Cat's Cradle*. Both works create a comic yet disturbing vision of puny human beings lost in a chaotic labyrinth. Both works end unhappily for the exhausted protagonists; there is no last moment *deus ex machina* that would order or explain. And both works decline into nihilism. Yet, their responses to it are quite different.

In *Cat's Cradle*, the earth has been frozen over by the accidental release of "ice-nine." For the few survivors of the catastrophe, the situation is entirely hopeless. Rather than suggesting "we must cultivate our garden," Bokonon, the outlaw prophet, recommends this course of action:

> If I were a younger man, I would write a history of human stupidity; and I would climb to the top of Mount McCabe and lie down on my back with my history for a pillow; and I would take from the ground some of the blue-white poison that makes statues of men; and I would make a statue of myself, lying on my back, grinning horribly, and thumbing my nose at You Know Who.

Vonnegut's attitude is characteristic of black humorists whose works typically make no plans for living in an absurd universe. The best one can do is ridicule with mocking laughter a cosmos that condemns mankind to an absurd fate. Accordingly, to the bitter end Vonnegut unflinchingly preserves his acerbic whimsicality.

At the conclusion of *Candide* hope is also dead. Voltaire has earlier ruled out suicide, leaving his audience in a metaphysical void with the tedium of work as the only solace. Instead of the zany, albeit, black merriment which characterizes previous episodes, we are left with a mood of somber abdication, a mood altogether different from Vonnegut's ridiculousness. This tonal change in Voltaire's conclusion is in the spirit of existential literature rather than the literature of black humor. Both grapple with an absurd human condition, and both are concerned with how one perseveres. But whereas the existentialist is earnest in delineating the implications of the absurd, the black humorist sees the absurd world as an outrageous joke with laughter as the only viable solution. In the end, Voltaire is not satisfied with laughing into the void. Instead, he grits his teeth.

Playing on His Readers' Desires

Gail S. Reed

> Gail S. Reed argues that Voltaire's exploration of the ef-
> fect of evil on his characters results in "a fundamental
> rhythm of expectation and betrayal." Reed contends that
> evil causes betrayal, which in turn causes catastrophic
> results that force the characters to search for safety and
> security from betrayal, two basic human needs that
> Voltaire assumes the readers themselves desire. Thus,
> Voltaire is using his characters to reflect his readers'
> needs. Reed is a practicing psychoanalyst who has pub-
> lished several articles on psychoanalysis and literature.

Several of Voltaire's best known tales are similar in shape
and plot, apparent variations on an inner theme. *Zadig*
(1741), *Candide* (1759), and *L'Ingénu* (1767) all involve a
naïve or idealistic protagonist wandering the world in
search of a woman who had been denied him by fate and authority, grappling the while with the frustration imposed by
arbitrary and powerful men and carried out through their
often impersonal and cruel institutions. At the chronological
center of the tales *Candide* has an emotional impact lacking
in the others; it has been frequently asserted that it is the
product of personal crisis and represents the author's confrontation with the existence of evil. Philosophic and biographical implications aside, for these have been frequently
discussed elsewhere, what formal factors, absent in the
other tales, compel this impression of the impact of evil? . . .

A RHYTHM OF EXPECTATION AND FRUSTRATION

One is the organization of the plot. Beneath the distancing and
mitigating ironic tone which characterizes the narrator's presentation, the world of *Candide* is built upon a fundamental
rhythm of expectation and betrayal. *Candide* is a dialectic of de-

sire and punishment, of trust and the brutal deception of that trust. The hero, innocently desiring Cunégonde and faithfully believing his tutor, is cast out into a best of all possible worlds which proves a mutilating inferno. Despairing, cold, hungry, and penniless, he finds his flagging faith restored by two strangers who treat him to dinner—then brusquely trick him into military servitude where he is robbed of any modicum of individuality and freedom, and finally stripped of his skin in a beating. His fellow sufferer, the old woman, in her parallel journey through life, is deprived by murder of a princely husband at the moment when she joyously anticipates marriage, then ravished, enslaved, and made witness to the dismemberment of her mother and attendants. A eunuch she believes kind fortunately rescues her from the bloody pile of corpses onto which she has collapsed, then quickly sells her anew into slavery.

These betrayals, rhythmic norms rather than exceptions in *Candide*, frustrate fulfillment; within the fiction they break down the characters' integrity; without, they assault the reader's sense of security through continual frustration of his conventional expectations of the marvelous. The two travelers, so often brutalized and betrayed, withdraw into a state of numbness in which, separate from their bodies, they feel neither physical nor emotional pain; they merely endure. Candide wordlessly traverses a war-torn countryside, objective correlative to his burnt-out inner state; the old woman, less and less desired, becomes first concubine, then slave, then an object dispatched from city to city, until her body is reduced to its most concrete physicality and becomes food. In a final bitter irony, buttock replaces breast in a gruesome parody of the primordial experience of security.

One result of this catastrophic rhythm is the intensified search for warmth and safety. The main characters yearn for protection, for a magic circle of comfort, security, and satiety, as is attested to by their frequent hunger, their stubborn innocence and comic grandiosity, their idealization of Westphalia, and their constant and oft contradicted assertions that they are infallible, perfect, or deserving of the best. Characters and reader are temporarily granted that protection in Eldorado.

EVIL IN THE OUTSIDE WORLD

Another and parallel result is the release of destructive forces. Indeed the fictional reality of the tale does not permit retreat for long. Outside that magic circle of perfection resides the social world into which the characters are constantly propelled. And this evil outside world is a place where the social institution seeks out the individual to destroy him. Children are castrated to sing in operas, slaves dismembered for disobedience, the military takes brutal possession of Candide's body. In fact, the double row of soldiers poised to club him becomes a giant devouring maw. In this evil social world, rationalized sadism runs rampant. There are, of course, the overt acts of individuals who enslave, rob, rape, and disembowel, but the esthetically pleasing ritual of an auto-da-fé [burning of heretics] camouflages equally sadistic yet socially sanctioned wishes. When brutality is committed in the name of good, when justice condones robbery and charges a fee, when freedom involves a choice between death by clubbing or firing squad, then language becomes the agent of social deception and the social world beyond the magic circle a place of uncertain perception as well as of danger. Deceiving characters emerge from its midst conferring names on themselves, promising uniqueness and coveting riches, and then merge back into its anonymity. Thus the false Cunégonde is only "a cheat." Candide also becomes part of the universe of shifting forms—separated from his name—stepping back from naïve candor into the socially conferred guise of mercenary. In rapid succession he offers his loyalty to the Spanish, then the Jesuits, avows his German birth and finds Cunégonde's brother, then disguises himself as Jesuit in order to flee, and is held prisoner and threatened with death by the Oreillons because accoutrements designate him as Jesuit. He escapes with his life only by slipping out of the clothing of his assumed identity. This social world, representing the individual's rage at frustration, destroys the self. In becoming part of its spreading insubstantiality, the individual momentarily ceases to exist.

One way in which the evil realm incorporates the self is by undermining the individual's perceptions and thus depriving him of his ability to anticipate, judge, and experience himself as a subjective continuity in time. Encountering Candide, the major characters emerge out of the treacherous social world in continuously changing shapes. The "femme tremblante, d'une taille majestueuse, brillante de pierreries, et couverte d'une voile"[1] is Cunégonde, though the other veiled woman is a fraud. One of the women "qui

1. trembling figure of a majestic-looking woman, all sparkling with jewels and hidden by a veil

124 Readings on Candide

étendaient des serviettes sur des ficelles pour les faire sécher"² is also Cunégonde "rembrunie, les yeux éraillés, la gorge sèche, les joues ridées, les bras rouges & écaillés."³ The commander, "le bonnet à trois cornes en tête, la robe retroussée, l'épée au côté, l'esponton à la main,"⁴ is the young Baron. He metamorphoses into friend, then into arrogant aristocrat, changes effected with a chameleon-like speed paralleled by Candide's confusion of names: "'Mon révérend père, . . . mon ancien maître, mon ami, mon beau-frère.'"⁵ Pangloss reappears as an ineffective galley-slave, as a corpse dissected back to life, and most frighteningly as that phantom who throws himself on Candide:

> un gueux tout couvert de pustules, les yeux morts, le bout du nez rongé, la bouche de travers, les dents noires, & parlant de la gorge, tourmenté d'une toux violente, & crachant une dent à chaque effort.⁶

The destructiveness represented by the instability of the social realm and of the self here intersect, for Pangloss' ghostly "disguise" is a mutilation which ordinarily belongs to nightmare. By making disguise a matter of body, the text turns the possible illusion of the ghost into the fictional reality of a disfigured tutor. As the physical body yields its integrity, the character becomes his disguise, becomes, that is, other.

Both the savageness of the fictional reality and the rhythm of the plot depend on the radical simplicity of the hero for their full effect. An appropriate accompaniment to the cruel and unstable reality which surrounds him, the characteristics united by the name of Candide designate him incomplete. The oscillations of his spirits according to the fullness of his stomach, his taking in of Pangloss' teachings because of the facilitating presence of the beautiful Cunégonde, his profound dependence on her to give his life shape and direction, his belief that a high degree of happiness consists in *being* her, all suggest that Voltaire has constructed a developmentally primitive literary character. So much, in fact, is Candide's simplicity coupled with devices which suggest infantile experience, that it shocks us to discover in the last chapter that as he has reached maturity he has acquired a beard.

2. who is hanging towels out on a line to dry 3. all brown, with her eyes bloodshot, her bosom shrivelled, her cheeks wrinkled, and her arms red and peeling 4. with the three-cornered hat on his head, his cassock hitched up, a sword at his side, and a halberd in his hand 5. Dear God, . . . my former master, my friend, my brother-in-law. 6. a beggar all covered with sores; his eyes were glazed, the end of his nose was eaten away, his mouth was askew, his teeth black, and he spoke from the back of his throat. He was wracked by a violent cough and spat out a tooth with every spasm.

Despite this growth—for much of the tale Candide is so lacking in self-definition that he is . . . devoid of judgment. Thus, he is dependent on guides to judge for him. Whether they prove trustworthy, like Cacambo, or treacherous, like Venderdendur, is a hazard of his radical simplicity, for his lack of differentiation manifests itself in uncritical, open-mouthed, passive receptivity.

It is this infantile openness, moreover, that involves the reader in the fictional world and thus in its brutal betrayals. Nothing masks Candide's primitive yearning for Cunégonde, or for that best world promised by Pangloss, and these wishes, emerging contrapuntally against the cruel deceptions of the plot, tend to elicit the reader's empathic wishes for food, warmth, and protection. Thus, when Candide's are abruptly frustrated, so too, our own.

THE READER AND THE TEXT

The reader's subjective participation in Candide's desires is facilitated in a number of ways. Among the most important is the adroit use of "internal focus" [French scholar Gerard] Genette's term for the restriction of the reader's field of vision to that of a given character. Of course, internal focus is not the norm of *Candide* where the narration, like that of most tales, is omniscient. Rather, internal focus represents a temporary shift of perspective away from narrative omniscience. Sometimes nearly imperceptible, such a shift may also involve the reader quite dramatically and subjectively in fictional danger. Immediately after the safe arrival in Buenos Aires where Cunégonde and Candide have fled together, new danger supervenes.

> Elle court sur le champ à *Candide.* "Fuyez," dit-elle, "ou dans une heure vous allez être brûlé." Il n'y avait pas un moment à perdre; mais comment se séparer de *Cunégonde*, & où se réfugier?[7]

Objective description cedes to an internal focus upon Candide's experience of his predicament. At this point, the chapter ends, the danger unresolved and under-distanced.

The reader's vision is reduced to a restricted internal focus that limits his knowledge of the fictional world as severely as Candide's and renders him equally helpless. Thus the reader becomes temporarily one with a character of nei-

---

7. Whereupon she rushed off to Candide: "Quick, off you go," she said, "or in an hour you'll be burnt." There was not a moment to lose. But how could he leave Cunegonde, and where was he to hide?

ther judgment nor knowledge, and the force of that sadistic reality through which the child-hero is deprived of wished-for security increases. The sense of helplessness is complemented by the frustration of the chapter break, a device which, as a formal analogue to Candide's sense of being trapped, places the reader in the same position of power-lessness in relation to the narrator as the hero finds himself in vis-à-vis the causal events of the fiction. . . .

What spares the reader too much disorientation is the distancing effect of the omniscient narration. The narrator, reliable, objective, in control, gives a counterbalancing stability to the unstable fictional world and authority to the events he describes. The breadth and scope of his vision creates a distance from fictional event which permits the reader the anticipation of danger, the illusion of safety, and the luxury to appreciate irony. With this broader perspective, the narrator exposes the naiveté of Candide and the self-importance of his companions, enabling us, [thank God], to find release in laughter.

Yet this relief is not so complete as we might suspect. It alleviates, but does not prevent, our subjective reaction to the dangers of the fictional world. In the presentation of the earthquake, for instance, disaster strikes mimetically:

> A peine ont-ils mis le pied dans la ville en pleurant la mort de leur bienfaiteur, qu'ils sentent la terre trembler sous leurs pas; la mer s'élève en bouillonnant dans le port, & brise les vaisseaux qui sont à l'ancre.[8]

The restrained description of upheaval in and of itself hardly moves. Rather, its placement in a sequence in which natural disaster and human cruelty follow each other precipitously surprises. When Plangloss and Candide set foot on shore after the death of Jacques and the shipwreck, reader and characters alike prepare for a respite. But safety is accorded only an introductory subordinate clause—in the main clause new disaster shocks.

Only after the reader is startled into subjectivity, does the narrative present the exaggerated and idiosyncratic reactions of the victims: the sailor looks for booty, Pangloss for a way of justifying his philosophic system, Candide for solace. Shock is countered by comedy. Yet these stylized descriptions are dependent on the reader's initial surprise for their comic effect. They afford him release secondarily because

8. Scarcely had they set foot in the city, still weeping over the death of their benefactor, than they felt the earth quake beneath their feet. In the port a boiling sea rose up and smashed the ships lying at anchor.

they allow him to escape his subjective involvement and to regard the beleaguered characters objectively.

Nor is the earthquake scene an exception. For the first half of the tale, over and over again, deftly and economically, the narrative moves the reader from safety to new danger: Candide and Cunégonde tell leisurely and objectively of the horrors of their lives in the comfort of a sea journey only to be separated the moment they come to port. Further, the narrative moves the reader from safe objectivity to the intimacy of the subjective not only by means of such formal devices as shifts of focus and manipulation of chapter divisions, but also by means of a play with convention which turns the events of the fiction into versions of chance as haphazard and out of control as the fictional world itself.

The rhythm of trust and betrayal, safety and danger thus finds its counterpart in the oscillation of the reader between participation in the danger of the fictional world and a more comfortable sharing of the omniscient narrator's objectivity. Until Candide begins to grow in the second half of the tale, his radical simplicity, evoking as it does a universal infantile defenselessness, emerges as a crucial subjective focus from which objective narration must rescue us before the boundaries of comedy are transgressed.

Through the structure of the text, then, the reader of *Candide* is engaged in a cycle of wish, frustration, and reactive anger which facilitates a transient identification with an infantile hero, on the one hand, and lends the impact of anger to the arbitrary external authority which assails him, on the other. The plot itself and formal elements such as the ordering of the action, the handling of narrative focus, and the syntax all contribute to the reader's identificatory wishes for warmth, safety, and security. When these wishes, apparently realized, are abruptly frustrated, the resultant anger fosters an experience of outside authority—whether fictional destiny or social institution—as cruel and implacable. The power which anger confers upon frustrating authority, in turn, increases the experience of powerlessness through which the reader, identified with the hero/victim, confronts his own vulnerability. Thus the transient identification with the hero is reinforced and the cycle of wish, frustration, and anger renewed. This reciprocal relationship between literary structure and the affect—conscious or not—that that structure evokes in the reader is an essential and complex element in the esthetic experience of *Candide*.

CHAPTER 4

Human Nature as Seen in Voltaire's Characters

Women's Equality in *Candide*

Arthur Scherr

In this selection, Arthur Scherr examines Voltaire's treatment of his female characters in *Candide*. Scherr, a history and English instructor at Bernard Baruch College and the City University of New York, has published a number of scholarly articles. Here, he argues that Voltaire has created women characters who are the "moral, intellectual, and physical" equals of men. While the men of the novel tend to argue over trifles, judge harshly and cynically, and act illogically, *Candide*'s women show a great deal of common sense, strength, and fairness in judgment.

Candide, Voltaire's great philosophical *conte* [story], is undoubtedly among the most popular and perennial of literary works; as such it has received an enormous share of frequently esoteric critical attention. Invariably stressing the climactic final chapter, concluding with Candide's decisive pronouncement, "il faut cultiver notre jardin" [we must cultivate our garden], many interpretations center on the issue of theodicy and the extent to which Voltaire and his protagonist recommend active struggle against evil, oppression, and war rather than isolated, selfish withdrawal from an inhumane society. Though these questions are important, *Candide* may be read on a parallel level as an examination of gender relationships and as Voltaire's paean to the beauty, common sense, intelligence, and resourcefulness of women. An argument for the moral, intellectual, and physical equality of women and men, interdependent composites of strength and frailty confronting an indifferent, often harsh natural environment and a brutal, indeed malevolent social one, is among its themes.

In Voltaire's own life women played a far greater role than men. Though he never married, Voltaire readily acknowl-

Excerpted from Arthur Scherr, "Voltaire's *Candide:* A Tale of Women's Equality," *Eighteenth-Century Studies*, Spring 1993, vol. 34, no. 3, pp. 261–282. Copyright © 1993 American Society for Eighteenth-Century Studies. Reprinted with permission from Johns Hopkins University Press.

edged his dependence on his two mistresses, Marquise du Châtelet (1706–1749) and Mme Denis (1712–1790), who was also his niece, for intellectual, emotional, and erotic sustenance. They were his confidantes; indeed, the scholarly Emilie Le Tonnelier de Breteuil, Marquise du Châtelet—whom he lived with at her château at Cirey for much of the period from 1734–1749—inspired his enthusiasm for Newtonian physics, the philosophical study of history, metaphysics, biblical criticism, and deism. . . .

Both Voltaire's personal life and his *chef d'oeuvre, Candide,* attest his respect for women's experience and his belief in equality and reciprocity between the sexes. Both genders endure parallel ordeals, conflicts, and challenges and meet them with a common fortitude. At several junctures Cunégonde, Paquette, and the Old Woman more aptly reflect Voltaire's buoyant, "bisexual" temperament than the men, who invariably, like Candide and Pangloss, engage in passionate defense of absurd philosophical dogmas; argue illogically, often in an unwittingly droll and ironic manner, like the young Baron expounding his aristocratic prerogatives; or cynically evaluate people and events, like Pococuranté and Martin. At least until the final chapter, when Candide invokes the need to "cultivate our garden," the novel's women display greater common sense, resilience, assertiveness, and sincerity. . . .

STRENGTH OF THE FEMALE CHARACTERS

The Old Woman's . . . courage and clearheadedness in the face of danger reveal the strength of the female character. She speaks some of the *conte's* most eloquent dialogue, whose message encompasses the human condition in general, rather than women alone. Despite her suffering, she tells Candide, "I still loved life. This ridiculous weakness is perhaps one of our most baleful inclinations; for is there anything more foolish than to want to bear continually a burden that one steadily wants to throw to the ground? To hold one's being in horror, and to cling to one's being? In a word, to caress the snake that devours us until it has eaten our heart?" These poetic words show the Old Woman's poignant understanding of what Enlightenment thinkers like Hume called the underlying, "constant and universal principles of human nature." She expresses a sense of resignation to her abysmal fate more characteristic, in eighteenth-century

fiction, of a venerable *male* sage than a woman. Voltaire
again subtly demonstrates his confidence in the intellectual
and moral equality of the sexes—through the unlikely, pa-
thetic figure of the Old Woman.

At this point in the *conte*, Candide's intellectual timidity
sharply contrasts with the Old Woman's bold espousal of
universal truths. Still too insecure to challenge his tutor Pangloss's inane Optimism, he feebly admits that, even with his
new awareness of moral and physical evil, were he now to
encounter his old teacher he would merely "feel enough
strength in me to dare, respectfully, to make some objec-
tions." However, Candide shares his strange old female
counterpart's ambiguity toward life: exemplifying the verac-
ity of her statements, he laments his existence and wishes for
death, all the while gorging himself with food as his valet Cacambo proposes after their escape from the Paraguayan Jesuits. As psychoanalyst Gail Reed implies, he behaves much
like "his fellow sufferer, the old woman, in his parallel journey through life," who regrets her fate yet continues ea-
gerly—voraciously?—to live. Voltaire again expounds the
uniformity of human nature—old and young, male and female.

In other ways Candide has retained compassionate, "feminine" values. When he travels in the New World and observes a mutilated slave who informs him of injustices perpetrated against him both by his African parents and Dutch
slave-traders, Candide weeps at the sight, once and for all renouncing Panglossian optimism. Unable to control his emo-
tions, "his heart was on his lips" and he bluntly expressed
his horror.

Yet, despite his excursions into metaphysics, Candide remains a man of passion as well as compassion. His obses-
sive love for Cunégonde may be only a temporary romantic
fetish, the product of his youth and limited sexual experience; indeed, he is willingly seduced by a Parisian marquise
who runs a gambling house, although he feels pangs of guilt
over his infidelity. Nevertheless, when he fails to find Cunégonde on his arrival in Venice he grows so despondent that
he is rendered temporarily impotent and sinks into a "black
melancholy." Candide's infantile dependence on his fantasized image of her reveals he still has a long way to go before reaching maturity. At least until the final chapter of the
novel, when he conceives the idea of "cultivating our gar-

den," he seems much less able than Cunégonde to cope with crises in a self-controlled manner.

DISGUST AT THE TREATMENT OF WOMEN

Voltaire's depiction of prostitutes and "kept women" in *Candide*, a theme which critics and historians have seldom noted or taken seriously, conveys his disgust at the system of sexual and physical exploitation inflicted upon them. Flagrantly enslaved by Moslem princes, and, albeit with the assistance of a thin veneer of propriety in European Christendom as well in the form of prostitution and legal prohibitions, women were deprived of social equality and opportunity. Such egregious injustices, Voltaire was well aware, denied women the right to fulfill their potential. The naive Candide is his vehicle for communicating this message. When he observes a robust monk arm-in-arm with a pretty young woman (another of Voltaire's slightly-concealed swipes at priestly asceticism), Candide gleefully asserts that their ostensible happiness refutes his comrade Martin's pessimism. To his chagrin, he soon discovers that the girl is none other than Pangloss's former mistress Paquette, now reduced to prostitution, work she says she despises, an "abominable trade which seems so pleasant to you men, and which is nothing but an abyss of misery for us." The reality of woman's sexual and economic oppression and degradation belies the mirthful appearance of the two lovers, who are actually merely a whore and her client. Perhaps most overwhelming for Candide is the fact that Paquette, formerly a maid in the barony of Thunder-ten-tronckh, like him exiled from the Castle as punishment for a sexual indiscretion, has been forced to resort to this lowly vocation. Far from fitting the stereotype of the lewd, insatiable vixen, Paquette, somewhat like Candide, is an ingenuous, amenable individual, victim of forces beyond her control, forced to sell her body in order to survive because this is one of the few options male society allowed women of her time. Like Candide, who bestows funds on Paquette as well as Friar Giroflée in a feeble effort to lighten their despair, we are prone to feel sympathy for the unfortunate young woman rather than disdain.

The Venetian senator Pococuranté, a member of the idle rich class who lived off unearned wealth in an aristocratic regime, furnishes an example of the odious and dishonest gender relations which pervade an inegalitarian society. Like many powerful men, the senator, reputedly a rich and carefree ruler, sexually exploited women in a futile attempt to fill the emotional void within him. Painting a realistic picture, not an idyllic one, with a frankness to equal Candide's Pococuranté admits that he sometimes sleeps with his serving girls rather than the "ladies of the town," who annoy him with "their coquetries, their jealousies, their quarrels, their moods, their pettinesses, their pride, their follies, and the sonnets one must write or order for them." Unfortunately, his scullions already bored him, a sign he would soon resume his courtship of "ladies" of higher social rank.

RECOGNIZING WORTH OVER BEAUTY

In contrast with the amoral Pococuranté, Candide's relationship with Cunégonde is a model of chivalry. Even after his valet Cacambo returns with news that she is now a slave of a deposed Hungarian prince at Constantinople, that "she has lost her beauty, and has become horribly ugly," Candide perseveres in his loyal determination to make her his wife: "Ah! beautiful or ugly, I'm an honorable man, and it's my duty to love her always." Though he would soon discover that such quixotism could be extremely painful and marries Cunégonde partly to spite her obdurate, aristocratic brother the Baron, Candide has more respect for women and empathy with their feelings than the insouciant Pococuranté and most of the other male characters, including, ironically, the scholar Pangloss, who views them solely as sex objects.

Candide finds Cunégonde and the Old Woman immured and working as drudges (*esclaves*) in Constantinople; no sooner do they discern their gentle liberator than they immediately reassert themselves and recover their self-esteem. Insisting that Candide fulfill his pledge to marry her as soon as he ransoms her from servitude, Cunégonde "did not know that she had grown ugly, nobody had told her so: she reminded Candide of his promises in so peremptory a tone that the good Candide did not dare refuse her." With this ironic sentence Voltaire conveys the poignant truth that, so long as women perceive their value as arising from others' opinion of their physical attributes, they will never recognize their real selves. Perhaps Cunégonde's new "ugliness," by permitting her to discover her worth as a social human being instead of a sexual object, may prove her salvation and path to happiness. Candide plays a crucial part in effecting her socialization, thereby underlining the reciprocal and symbiotic relationship which Voltaire envisages prevailing between the sexes in his ideal society, Candide's garden. Accepting her despite her withered look, he takes her for his wife, an eventually salutary outcome for both partners.

Candide's initial obsession with Cunégonde undoubtedly arises from physical attraction and the sensual experience with her before the Baron expels him from the Castle "with great kicks in the behind." As Douglas A. Bonneville perceptively observes, this first erotic contact with his idealized version of woman has an indelible impact on him, inciting his unrelenting pursuit of Cunégonde and furnishing the novel's *leitmotiv.* "The ascendancy of that idealized love over a virtually intolerable reality is absolutely essential to the novel," he points out. When Candide agrees to marry Cunégonde despite her revulsive appearance, he obeys an ethical imperative of duty that transcends his previous motivation. Although he feels "dehumanized" by the change that has come over his beloved, he rejects a nihilistic egotism and, fearful of irreparably damaging Cunégonde's feelings and self-esteem, becomes her spouse. In Bonneville's view, Candide's decisions at the end of the novel in marrying Cunégonde and settling down at Constantinople evince his growth into a sensitive and compassionate human being, "[and] may be viewed as the two great sacrifices that the feeling individual must make of himself, one to another person or persons, and the other to the community." On the other hand, since his search for Cunégonde has comprised Candide's *raison d'être* throughout the *conte,* it would seem that he had little option but to rejoin her and form a *petite société* with a handful of friends he had encountered since setting out on his journey of discovering life. Voltaire seems to suggest that men and women are interdependent on one another for their identities and self-fulfillment; Candide's obsession with reuniting with Cunégonde—a kind of lost "other self"—like the interchange of gender roles and characteristics that frequently occurs in the novel, indicates this to be among *Candide*'s themes.

THE ROLE OF WOMEN IN CANDIDE'S SELF-REALIZATION

Candide is dependent on women for self-realization in other ways as well. Indeed, the Old Woman, like Cunégonde, pro-

vides the impetus for his discovery of the garden whose cultivation gives his life meaning at the novel's conclusion. Despite her ugliness and servile status, the Old Woman does
not demur at instructing Candide on the proper manage-
ment of his money after he purchases her freedom: "There
was a little farm in the neighborhood; the old woman suggested to Candide that he acquire it until the whole group
should enjoy better fortunes." Just as the Old Woman,
proposing that he buy the farm which makes possible a
tranquil ending to Candide's tale, significantly contributes to
the little community's progress, Cunégonde's timely original
seductive acts at the outset of the *conte,* by precipitating his
exile from the bogus paradise of Castle Thunder-ten-
tronckh, willy-nilly incited his *Bildung* in quest of the good
life, whose terminus was the garden "paradise" to which the
Old Woman directed him. Women take the initiative and
play key roles in these two decisive events of Candide's life:
the younger in his removal from a sham, corrupted idyll,
commencing his voyage to self-awareness; the elder in en-
sconcing him on his own ground where he might live au-
tonomously and find a semblance of peace. Voltaire thereby
hints at female complicity, like Eve's in the proverbial Garden of Eden, in facilitating Candide's entry into his own rus-
tic "paradise."

Along with the Jews, woman are among the egregiously
oppressed social groups, both in Europe and the Islamic
world, that are instrumental in assisting Candide's discovery
and settlement of his utopian community. Jewish merchants
provided the funds and the Old Woman pointed the way to
the demesne which symbolizes a society and culture in
which they would invariably achieve greater freedom and
self-respect than under feudal polities: the liberal bourgeois
state. Candide's female companions exercise their freedom
to express disappointment at the *métairie's* failure to achieve
an impossible dream—the luxurious, engaging, and at the
same time carefree existence they desire. His nagging wife
Cunégonde, "growing uglier every day, grew shrewish and
insufferable [*insupportable*]," while "the old woman was ail-
ing and was even more ill-tempered than Cunégonde." Yet
stoical Candide willingly tolerates their complaints—deem-
ing them as valid as those of the "overworked" farm laborer
Cacambo and the disgruntled philosopher Pangloss, who
laments his nondescript status—denoting the increased so-

cial influence of women in the burgeoning capitalist structure symbolized by the *petit jardin.* He respects the women's wisdom, empathizes with their misfortunes, and recognizes the authenticity of their experience.

A COMPASSION FOR WOMEN

The reaction of the male members of the little community to the return of Paquette and her companion Friar Giroflée, recent escapees from prison, reasserts their compassion for women and their recognition that they were forced into prostitution by the paucity of vocations available to them in the white male-dominated hierarchy of the time. Though Paquette reports that, she and her friend (possibly also her pimp) Friar Giroflée having exhausted Candide's gift, she had "continued her trade everywhere, and no longer earned anything with it," the men welcome rather than ostracize her, the latter a common occurrence during the eighteenth century when prostitutes were frequently denied even a decent burial. Though the satyr Pangloss suspects that Paquette had infected him with syphilis during their earlier frolics at the Castle, even he pities her degraded condition. As C.J. Betts has noted, Pangloss's encounter with the waiflike Paquette, more than any other event in the novel, leads him to doubt the validity of the dogma of Optimism and a beneficent Providence to which he had been so inexorably devoted. "Ah! Ah! So heaven brings you back among us here, my poor child!" he exclaims when he meets her in Candide's garden. "Do you know that you cost me the end of my nose, an eye, and an ear? Now look at you! Eh! What a world this is!" Paquette's and Giroflée's vicissitudes, money's failure to bring happiness either to the man or the woman, only deepen the perplexity of the members of the *petite société.*

The group's apathy appears to be resolved by Candide's directive, after visiting the industrious Turkish farmer and his two sons and two daughters, that "we must cultivate our garden." This aphorism pithily expresses Voltaire's own view that life's meaning is founded on both genders' pursuit of individual autonomy, productivity, and simultaneous symbiosis and self-reliance. The narrator draws the larger significance of the *conte's* finale, acclaiming Candide's "praiseworthy plan," which should enable each member of the community "to exercise his [or her] talents."

WOMEN'S VALUE TO THE COMMUNITY

Women, like men in Candide's sexually egalitarian society, have their unique function, a role equally essential to the community's survival. The erstwhile beautiful baroness Cunégonde and her former maid, the ex-prostitute Paquette, find themselves social equals on a *métairie* where only efficient labor counts. Cunégonde decides to make use of her *métier de cuisiniére* (vocation as a cook), the only skill this ex-aristocrat possessed, which, ironically, she learned during her enslavement by the Bulgarians. Like the other members of Candide's community, she will employ her abilities for the sustenance and enhancement of the group. As the narrator informs us:

> The little property produced much. True, Cunégonde was very ugly, but she became an excellent pastry cook; Paquette embroidered; the old woman took care of the linen. Not even Friar Giroflée failed to perform some service; he was a very good carpenter, and even became respectable.

In Candide's cooperative yet individualistic community, woman is an active participant rather than merely an object of male lust. Though Friar Giroflée, Paquette's companion, had wasted his life in profligacy, now both were involved in productive enterprises. Candide's community has reformed the manifold corruptions of the Old Régime, which it replaces with a middle-class paradise in which human exploitation and injustice—sexual, economic, and religious—are uprooted and profitable labor esteemed the standard of value. Himself a successful scientific farmer on his Genevan estate at Les Délices and his French properties at Ferney, Voltaire expounds the Protestant, bourgeois work ethic of modern capitalism in *Candide* in the metaphoric guise of commercial farming.

Of equal significance with her social role, in Candide's garden, woman's self-image—her consciousness, to use a modern term—is transformed. This is not to deny that Cunégonde's personality has undergone steady maturation throughout the *conte*; perhaps more than any other character, she has *grown* through suffering. It is important to keep in mind that in the beginning, she is a recognized member of the nobility, with all the privileges accruing to that caste. Like Candide, she is imbued with belief in the infallibility of Panglossian Optimism. Nevertheless, she is disabused of this vacuous notion much earlier than her paramour, asserting, when she sees Candide flogged and his tutor hanged by the Inquisition, "Pangloss, then, most cruelly deceived me when he told me that all is for the very best." Candide himself, overwhelmed by her majestic beauty and elegance, "obeyed her with profound respect" when they encounter each other in Lisbon. She learns a stoic endurance of suffering that hardens her to the exploitation she experiences for three months at the hands of the Bulgarian captain. Despite her religious upbringing, Cunégonde transcends the prejudices of her time sufficiently to feel indignant at the evils of the "barbaric" Inquisition and to be "seized with horror" at the murder of the Jews. In Cunégonde's speech describing to Candide her thoughts and feelings at witnessing the *auto-da-fé* [burning of heretics], Voltaire mingles a note of sublime pathos with the satire, indicating his sympathy rather than hostility or derision of women:

> Agitated, bewildered, sometimes beside myself and sometimes ready to die of faintness, I had my mind full of the massacre of my father, of my mother, of my brother, the insolence of my vile Bulgarian soldier [who raped her], of the knife cut he gave me, of my slavery, of my trade as cook, of my Bulgarian captain . . . of the hanging of Doctor Pangloss . . . and above all of the kiss I had given you behind the screen the day I had seen you for the last time. I praised God, who was leading you back to me through so many trials.

Cunégonde is no longer a callow seventeen-year-old, as she was at the beginning of the novel, but a sensitive and prudent young woman, who, more precociously than Candide, survives her ordeals, and extracts humility and empathy with others out of her own suffering, surmounting her earlier adolescent naiveté.

GENDER EQUALITY

On the other hand, for much of the novel, in fact until their arrival at Candide's garden, the women—Paquette, Cunégonde, even the grotesque Old Woman—resignedly acquiesce, though not without an occasional murmur of protest, in the status of sexual objects which male culture has bestowed on them. Conversely, the ethos of Candide's "Garden of Eden," as Pangloss indirectly refers to it, denigrates the feudal-theocractic and sexually oppressive societies of both the Christian and Moslem worlds. Even the Turkish farmer's daughters in chapter thirty are unduly obsequious as they "perfume the beards" of Candide, Pangloss, and Martin, a token of woman's subjugation to the male. By contrast, the women in Candide's garden are in no way relegated to an inferior position: resourcefully and maturely utilizing skills she learned during her captivity, Cunégonde becomes an "excellent pastry cook," hardly a degrading occupation and one carried on by men as well as women. Paquette and the Old Woman are employed in clothing the group; if they are subjected to drudgery, it is no worse than that of the men, who are laboring on the farm as well.

Candide's final paragraph, part of which has been quoted above describing the occupations of the citizens of Candide's garden, epitomizes the *leitmotiv* of gender equality in a bourgeois paradise. Instructing the apparently indolent, persistently quixotic Pangloss, "we must cultivate our garden," Candide tersely distinguishes his community's moral code from that of the Old World: it differs profoundly from the regimen of rape, torture, and forced labor the women endured from the time of Cunégonde's captivity by the Bulgarians until Candide finally liberates her from her servitude to the deposed prince of Transylvania, whose shirts she washed in the hot sun. Cunégonde is no longer beautiful and hardly appealing as a sexual object—a harsh disappointment to Candide, who has fantasized about her in this manner, notwithstanding an illusory romantic veneer, for most of the novel until he observes her wizened appearance, the result of physical, sexual, and psychic abuse under both Christian and Moslem masters. In the new, middle-class Garden of Eden her merit arises neither from her noble lineage nor her sensual charms; she is accepted because of her productivity and to the extent she is willing to cooperate with others. Cunégonde has matured from a stagnant sexual or physical object, valued solely for the bodily pleasure she gave men or the amount of menial toil she performed for them, to an *individual* esteemed for the quality of her work and imbued with self-respect—pastry cook *par excellence* of Candide's garden. For this reason Bonneville seems unduly pessimistic in his somber conclusion that the tedium involved in her marriage to Candide symbolizes the universality of "woman's fate" and the deprivation of her former femininity: "True, she is spared childbirth, at least within the time span of the novel, but the banality of being a farmer's wife has neutered her as social function is said to neuter us all." Nevertheless, most of us ultimately discover that assuming unpleasant responsibilities is intrinsic to growing up and "putting away childish things," as St. Paul put it. Neither "femininity" nor "masculinity" is essential to living as productive individuals within Candide's halcyon community, nor is procreation a function incumbent on its women.

By the end of the novel, Candide himself no longer feels bound to adopt a "macho" *persona*, now that he is ensconced safely in a *gender-neutral* utopia. In distinct contrast to his earlier violence—killing the Grand Inquisitor and the Jewish merchant in Lisbon, shooting monkeys and attacking the Baron in South America, *sexual passion inspiring his behavior in each instance*—he plays a gentler, more peaceful role yet remains leader of the colony. Incorporating both passive and aggressive, "feminine" and "masculine" traits, he renounces brute force, accepting the ambiguities of his personality, facilitating his (and Voltaire's) psychic well-being. For Candide as for his comrades, the middle-class Garden of Eden promotes sexual equality and freedom and encourages the development of human potentialities.

Like the infant's transitory *in-utero* bond with the mother, Candide's first "paradise," Castle Thunder-ten-tronckh, microcosm of an Old Régime in decline, is soon violently eradicated. Though ejected like Adam from Paradise, Candide's "Fall," precipitated by his "sin" with "Eve" Cunégonde—the act of consenting sexual equals despite an absurd disparity in aristocratic lineage—brings about his "resurrection" through discovery of an alternative, more authentic, "bourgeois" Garden of Eden. Here Cunégonde and the Old Woman join him as a partners, not subjugated pawns like their sisters. Together with Paquette, Martin, Giroflée, Cacambo, and (albeit to a lesser extent) Pangloss, they symbolize the new power of the woman and the commoner in Voltaire's projected sexually egalitarian society.

Candide the "Dunce-king"—Exploring Evil Through a Band of Fools

Roy S. Wolper

In this article, Roy S. Wolper argues that Voltaire never intended to present his own philosophies through the character of Candide, but instead presents his views ironically through his characters' idiocy. Candide is a "Dunce-king" who is little more than a puppet, and Voltaire uses him and the others to explore the ties between "stupidity and evil." Wolper, assistant professor of English at Temple University, has published several essays on literature of the eighteenth century.

Too much of the recent criticism of *Candide* has a magisterial certainty about it. [Voltaire scholar] William F. Bottiglia, whose long analysis is now considered "fundamental and convincing," believes that Voltaire "ends by affirming that social productivity of any kind at any level constitutes the good life, that there are limits within which man must be satisfied to lead the good life, but that within these he has a very real chance of achieving both private contentment and public progress." Bottiglia insists there is "something wrong" with those whose conclusions differ from his own; he has analyzed "everything that is *objectively*" in *Candide* (like the "progression [that] is *objectively*" in the three final gardens).

   Peter Gay, who gives *Candide* a section in his *Interpretation* of the Enlightenment [i.e. Gay's book *The Enlightenment: An Interpretation*], does not acknowledge opposing views. Neither his text nor his notes indicate the indecision and conflicting theories concerning structure, style, theme,

Excerpted from Roy S. Wolper, "Candide, Gull in the Garden," *Eighteenth-Century Studies*, Winter 1969, vol. 3, no. 2, pp. 265–277. Copyright © 1970 American Society for Eighteenth-Century Studies. Reprinted with permission from Johns Hopkins University Press.

characters; Gay confidently judges all aspects, from aesthetics (*Candide* is "a unified work of art which is flawless and complete") to the *conte's* [story's] ultimate meaning ("Change can come from recognition of limits and concentration on realities"). In shorter critiques, there are similar dogmatic generalizations. Concerning the *conte's* essence, for example introductions offer little doubt: the theme is "to be creative and constructive in an efficacious way, to fight injustice whenever reasonably feasible"; "un conseil de travail et d'effort: la métaphysique n'est que leurre et duperie, l'action est bonne et féconde."[1] And it is this way with Voltaire's biographers, journalistic or scholarly: *Candide's* theme is "Life is a bad bargain, but one can make the best of it"; "le jardin à cultiver est . . . un tonique suffisant pour l'activité humaine."[2] Literary historians also present quick evaluations: "Voltaire is driven in *Candide* to his old standby, utilitarianism, or useful work."

The reason for these summaries, perhaps, has been the certainty of Voltaire's presence. Most critics explicitly identify Candide at the end of his odyssey with Voltaire: "il faut cultiver notre jardin"[3] is "in fact . . . *Voltaire's* solution" or "*Voltaire's* . . . message to man." Those who see Candide's final choice as a symbol of resignation and retreat or of social action support their views with biographical considerations. Norman L. Torrey feels that *Candide* "sums up the period of personal discouragement after [Voltaire's] departure from Berlin until his settlement near Geneva." For Gay, it is a transitional stage before commitment: "in the late 1750's . . . Voltaire still defined action as thoughtful resignation to reality." Bottiglia perceives a more positive attitude: Candide's course is parallel to Voltaire's, and in the 1750s Voltaire went from complacency, through pessimism, to "melioristic affirmation." Each theory finds a corner in biography, since Voltaire's life (like most others) had many substantial diverse tracks.

SEPARATING AUTHOR AND CHARACTER

Like the continual attempts to determine whether Candide's conclusions represent a retreat or a commitment to social action, such biographical inquiries perhaps obscure more

1. advice of work and effort: metaphysics is nothing but delusion and trickery, action is good and fertile 2. the garden to cultivate is . . . sufficient tonic for human activity 3. we must cultivate our garden

fundamental questions. For example, how do we know that Candide in the garden does speak and act for Voltaire? From the web of relevance of the *conte*, I suggest that in the garden Candide is speaking from *his* view of reality, not Voltaire's. There should be no great difficulty in accepting this hypothesis. Throughout, Candide has been the frequent and obvious butt of Voltaire's satire. Candide's easy gulling at the hands of the bedridden woman who pretended to be Cunégonde, his failure to restrain his appetite as he thought of murder and lost love and reputation, his "encore une fois, Pangloss avait raison, tout est bien"[4] once more, Pangloss was right, all is well (which occurs *after* many voyages in which Candide has seen cruelty and carnage, ecclesiastical and political and cultural stupidity)—all reveal Voltaire's clear detachment from his main character. At the very end, though free of Pangloss' optimistic certainty, isn't it possible that Candide, nevertheless, is a gull, as Zimri is a different son of Dulness from Achitophel, or as Sir Plume has a folly unlike Belinda's?

The structure of the *conte* that is usually accepted—the journey of the hero from naïveté to maturity—will not do. The reader cannot accept the conclusion that "the corps of experiences" led Candide to "conclusions of real consequence." Our awareness, which comes from the spread of meaningfulness within the *conte*, does not parallel Candide's. It is of a different order. . . . In *Candide*, it is the *reader* who perceives the nature and movement and source of evil; the multiple faces of Dulness and their interpenetration with vice; the shape and direction of a deterrent. Candide's epigrammatic conclusion, far from, as Bottiglia suggests, "summariz[ing] and unif[ying] the tale by answering the central problem," is irrelevant to it. Candide's limited vision is exemplified by his own triumph (of which, pertinently, he is unaware). He has fulfilled his earliest dreams: "Il concluait qu'après le bonheur d'être né baron de Thunder-ten-tronckh, le second degré de bonheur était d'être mademoiselle Cunégonde, le troisième, de la voir tous les jours; et le quatrième d'entendre maître Pangloss."[5] As hoe and shovel dig into the ground, Candide is the leader of the group, a surrogate

---

4. once more, Pangloss was right, all is well 5. His conclusion was that, next to the happiness of being born Baron Thunder-ten-tronckh, the second degree of happiness was being Miss Cunégonde, the third was seeing her every day, and the fourth was listening to Maître Pangloss.

baron Thunder-ten-tronckh; he is married to Lady Cuné-
gonde; and he has Pangloss as a constant conversationalist.
As a parody of the romantic hero who achieves his goal,
Candide is the mock-achiever, the Dunce-king—the "hero"
of the ironic mode. In this paper, then, I hope to suggest that
Candide's final generalization and his assumptions are not
Candide's wisdom. Candide's solution, I think, is not
Voltaire's. Through the technique of reduction, Voltaire sati-
rizes Candide as he has Cunégonde or Don Fernando
d'Ibaraa, y Figueora, y Mascarenes, y Lampourdos, y Souza.

The impulse to cultivate the garden is largely a result of
Candide's visit with the old Turk; afterwards, Candide "fit de
profondes réflexions" about the desirable life of the "bon
vieillard.". . .

[But] the old Turk clearly does not care about what happens any where save in his garden: "je n'ai jamais su le nom
d'aucun muphti, ni d'aucun vizir. J'ignore absolument
l'aventure dont vous me parlez . . . je ne m'informe jamais de
ce qu'on fait à Constantinople."[6] Mark Van Doren para-
phrases the assumption behind the thinking of the old Turk
and Candide: "No matter what Bulgaria or Turkey or England or France or Germany is doing, we are going to be safe
here." Yet the very location of the garden—in the Ma-
hometan world where life is cruel and barbarous—suggests
imminent danger. Moreover, Candide should know, and the
reader certainly is aware, that evil has no borders, and that
even the most innocent are often trammeled within its
mesh. Candide's band itself offers first-hand experience.
With no provocation, the old woman and Cunégonde were
raped and brutalized; the baron of Thunder-ten-tronckh had
his head smashed; the baroness was hacked to pieces; the
old woman's mother and her Italian attendants were
"déchirées" [torn up] and "coupées" [cut]. Candide saw the
senseless slaughter of innocent bystanders (the Portuguese
crypto-Jews, the three Westphalian boys, the fellow captives
of the old woman, the "honnête" [honest] Biscayan, and of
sizable populations (the inhabitants of the ransacked Avar
and Bulgar villages were raped and disemboweled; the citizens of Azov were massacred; in Morocco, "c'était un carnage continuel dans toute l'étendue de l'empire."[7] Perhaps

6. I never have known what any mufti or vizier was called. What you have just told me
means absolutely nothing to me. . . . I never inquire what's going on in Constantinople. 7. It was one long bloodbath from one end of the empire to the other.

the old Turk, within his twenty acres, has never seen the cancerous spread of evil, but Candide has. Candide's belief that safe gardens can continue in the world marks his blindness to experience; similarly, Pangloss' "tout est bien" [all is well] proves irrelevant to the dark realities around him. Both have missed the meaning of their travels. . . .

AVOIDING BOREDOM AND VICE

The "doctrine of work" which the little band practices is . . . , of course, a result of the old Turk; he tells Candide, "le travail éloigne de nous trois grands maux, l'ennui, le vice, et le besoin."[8] It has, seemingly, satisfied the old Turk's needs, and it appears a panacea for Candide's group since none contests it. Yet because of the Weltanschauung [perspective of life] that arises from the continual exposure of evils, the advice seems irrelevant. That it should be acted on by Candide underscores the superfluity of his group to the *conte*'s world.

FIGHTING BOREDOM

There is no doubt that the little band found boredom undesirable. The old woman openly says, "Je voudrais savoir lequel est le pire . . . d'éprouver enfin toutes les misères par lesquelles nous avons tous passé, ou bien de rester ici à ne rien faire?"[9] Candide admits, "C'est une grande question."[10] [Scholar] Robert Adams concludes that boredom "speaks more freely to Voltaire's condition, to Candide's, and to that of the human race"; it is "the real enemy against which work fights." It is known, moreover, that Voltaire dreaded boredom. Concerning vice, the second of the "grands maux" [great evils], the little band has been its victim so often that they know cultivating the ground does not involve them in exploiting people as economic or pleasurable objects. And they also have seen the unpleasantness of poverty. It denied Pangloss medical help; it made Candide an easy victim of the Bulgar recruiters; it led Paquette to prostitution, "un abîme de misère."[11] Martin generalizes about the importance of money, "j'étais fort pauvre: aussi n'eus-je ni amis, ni dévotes, ni médecins."[12]

---

8. work keeps us from three great evils: boredom, vice, and need   9. I would like to know which is worse . . . suffering all the misfortunes we've all suffered, or simply being stuck here doing nothing?   10. That is a good question.   11. a vale of tears   12. I was very poor, so I had no friends or do-gooders or doctors.

Yet such truths, the sensitive reader feels, are nevertheless irrelevant to *Candide*'s center. Although "le travail [work]" prevents "l'ennui [boredom]," how many of the hundreds in the *conte* suffer from that? The truncations of life that appear from Westphalia to Constantinople have so little to do with boredom that one can say that whatever the tale is essentially about, it is *not* the repercussions of "l'ennui." So too with "le besoin [need]." The profound and horrible suffering of the inhabitants is not due to poverty, since the impoverished do not have the power to impose injustice, punishment, or death on the innocent. What Adams calls "moral idiocy"—the cold indifference to life by the responsible leaders—is inextricably bound to the Establishment—to the business world of the Vanderdendurs, the legal world of bought magistrates, the religious world of inane dogma and quick persecution, the intellectual world of the University of Coimbra.

Vice, though, is important to the tale. In its largest sense, it is "le vice" which confronts Candide throughout his voyages and gives the *conte* its continuing grimness . . . yet is "le travail" an adequate deterrent? Although the old Turk and Candide and his group believe so, the reader knows it is not. Martin, for example, notes that in peaceful towns "les hommes sont dévorés de plus en plus d'envie, de soins et d'inquiétudes qu'une ville assiégée n'éprouve de fléaux."[13] Specifically, couldn't Issachar be a proficient banker for the court and still use Cunégonde? Couldn't the Dutch judge be knowledgeable and efficient, yet greedy? Couldn't the French surgeon, who is "fort adroit" [exceedingly adroit], lust after women? In *Candide*, those who work spread vice. Work cannot "éloigne" [drive away] vice, for work does not touch vice's nerve. Vice, to quote Montaigne again, "est principalement produit par bestile ignorance" [is principally produced by bestial ignorance].

Voltaire was aware of the close connection between stupidity and evil. In [his earlier novel] *Zadig*, for example, a ridiculous Arabian custom decrees that sanctification is attained through public self-immolation; inane tests for competence cause the expulsion of King Moabdar's dependable officials; secular thinking about the Celestial Host calls forth a sentence of death at the stake. Stupidity is virulent; it bruises and kills. To Voltaire, the cruel and the dumb are

13. men are devoured by more envy, worry, and dissatisfaction than all the scourges of a city under siege

kin—both the true faces of the same goddess, Dulness. Hence, the Pococurantes are relatives of the Vanderdendurs, the physician using Dioscoridean ointments is related to the rapacious pirate captain and to the sadistic Bulgar regimental officer; the academy at Bordeaux is a sister institution of the Catholic church. This, then, is the pulse that unifies *Candide*. The bumbling Pangloss personifies both currents. Pangloss, "le plus grand philosophe de la province,"[14] prevents Candide from saving the Anabaptist Jacques "en lui prouvant que la rade de Lisbonne avait été formée exprès pour que cet anabaptiste s'y noyât."[15]

And so the widely-quoted "doctrine of work" is not the *conte*'s wisdom. In fact, by adhering dully to it, the little group itself *contributes* to the ongoing cruelty and carnage: the produce from the garden will nourish the Vanderdendurs, the Gauchats, the Dutch judges, the Christian prelates, "Un million d'assassins enrégimentés, courant d'un bout de l'Europe à l'autre."[16] In effect, the yield supports and maintains the political, religious, cultural, and economic institutions of injustice. This point is made explicitly by the black slave who works on the sugar plantation: "l'usage" controls his slavery and dictates the punishment that deprives him of a hand and a leg. He tells Candide, "C'est à ce prix que vous mangez du sucre en Europe."[17] Like Vanderdendur's sugar, Candide's yield (as well as that of the old Turk) contributes to the exploitation of man by man. In *Candide*... "Universal Darkness" fills the sky of those who caponize children and of those who cultivate gardens. . . .

VOLTAIRE'S USE OF REDUCTION

Though Candide has rejected Pangloss' advice, nevertheless he is a dunce. Voltaire's technique is one common to satire—reduction. Throughout most of the tale, Candide is Pangloss' puppet, mouthing his old master's clichés regardless of circumstance. At the end, too, he is a marionette, but this time the old Turk is the puppeteer. To choose the garden is to reduce the rich awarenesses of the *conte*'s world to an oversimplified formula; to follow the old Turk's regimens—like "je ne m'informe jamais de ce qu'on fait à Constantinople"[18]

14. the greatest philosopher in the province 15. arguing that Lisbon harbour had been created expressly so that the Anabaptist would be drowned in it 16. one million regimented assassins, rushing from one end of Europe to the other 17. This is the price you pay for the sugar you eat in Europe. 18. I never enquire what's going on in Constantinople

148 of Readings on

or "le travail éloigne de nous trois grand maux, l'ennui, le vice, et le besoin"[19]—is to close one's eyes to the suffering of one's neighbor, to naively believe that appetitive evil can be fenced out, to blindly miss the grim implications of stupidity, to leave unfulfilled the growth of human potential. Candide's reductive solution is framed by an initial oversimplification: "Ce bon vieillard me paraît s'être fait un sort bien préférable à celui des six rois."[20] Why these two groups only? Why these two groups at all? And at the conclusion, the repetition of "il faut cultiver notre jardin" dramatically illustrates the contraction within the leader's mind. . . . Enclosed in a garden, an island amidst a world of brutality and carnage, Candide repudiates Pangloss' myth with paltry generalization.

Candide's group has been reduced to little more than functions. For a few, I think, this is not completely unfortunate. Paquette and Giroflée, who misspent their early lives, are better off: as an embroiderer, Paquette is neither passing on the falsity of hypocritical love nor the infection of venereal disease; as a carpenter, Giroflée is not using girls or spreading lies. But the others, I think, fare less well. Because Cunégonde has lost her beauty, she is, at the end, "acariâtre et insupportable."[21] Being an "excellente pâtissière"[22] does not enable her to see beyond concerns of the skin. (One should add that her occupation is especially apt since Candide's concern is his stomach.) The old woman who, in spite of debilitating assaults, could say, "j'aimais . . . la vie" [still I loved life] is, at the conclusion, in "mauvaise humeur." In her case, notwithstanding her useful chore of managing the linens, the serpent Life seems to have "mangé le coeur." Pangloss, Martin, and Candide, who are not seen at labor, have been called "the intellectual subgroup"; but with their pragmatic "doctrine of work," it is questionable whether any of the three philosophers has any subsequent function. The lack of such would not silence Pangloss. In the garden, his stock of examples illustrates "Tous les événements sont enchaînés dans le meilleur des mondes possibles"[23] as it has earlier substantiated the beneficence of Columbus' exporting of syphilis. He is an indefatigable prattler. Martin, whose cynicism has supported Candide's conclusion, demolishes

19. work keeps us from three great evils: boredom, vice, and need 20. That kind old man seems to me to have made a life for himself which is much preferable to that of those six kings. 21. shrewish and impossible to live with 22. excellent pastry-cook 23. all events form a chain in the best of all possible worlds

theorizing with his final speech, "Travaillons sans raison-ner"; "'c'est le seul moyen de rendre la vie supportable."[24] This itself, of course, is a theory and one that has not grown out of the travels of the adventurers. Candide, as the leader, has the primary responsibility of decision; his failure, and I take his conclusion to be such (is not the final proof Pan-gloss' agreement with him?), is due to his inability to under-stand Dulness and her brutish appetite.

Candide's band, then, does not embody the *conte*'s hope. Since Dulness is consistently portrayed as "le vice," the pos-itive force in *Candide* is virtue (in its largest sense). Implicit in virtue is the consideration of *other*, not self; the *world*, not the little group only. In the article on "Vertu" in the *Diction-naire Philosophique*, "L'HONNÊTTE HOMME" says, "la bienfai-sance est . . . la seule vraie vertu" [charity is . . . the only true virtue]. Except for Eldorado (most of the time), *Candide* dra-matizes the antithesis of beneficence—a kaleidoscope of people turning their backs on others except when using them in economic or religious or physical exploitation. As Pangloss has not learned much about the world, so Candide has learned little about virtue. Although he has taken in friends, he has not *advanced* in his generosity. In fact, ini-tially, he was more generous: he helped strangers, not asso-ciates. For example, he gave his last florins to the beggar-Pangloss (whom he had not recognized), and he pitched in and helped the survivors of the earthquake. In the more idyl-lic Eldorado, charity is everywhere. Even strangers receive the ready generosity of ample food, good quarters, and un-conditional help.

In the "real" world, only the charitable Anabaptist Jacques helps all whom he can—an impoverished Candide, an ill Pangloss, a drowning sailor. Ironically, the Bulgar re-cruiter who preys on the innocent says, "les hommes ne sont faits que pour se secourir les uns les autres" [man was made that he might help his fellow-man]. In that direction only lies the hope of the *conte*; the adventures insist on the need of beneficence to "un être, à deux pieds sans plumes, qui avait une âme" [a living being with two feet, no feathers, and possessed of a soul]. If one is charitable, there is no guaran-tee of a better world or of personal happiness. People like Jacques sometimes drown. But the *conte* is concerned nei-

24. Let's get down to work and stop all this philosophizing; it's the only way to make life bearable.

ther with sudden earthquakes nor with the fate of Jacques, but with the spirit Jacques has: to know whose head is impaled at the Sublime Porte and whose body is cast on the dunghill; to care about those who are poor; to educate those in government and religion and culture who hold to inane (and hence cruel) archaisms. These are *Candide*'s values, not Candide's. At the end, Candide, reduced to petty revenge, sells Cunégonde's brother into a galley, where Candide knows the baron will be whipped on his "épaules nuës" [bare shoulders].

Voltaire's View of Degenerate Man

A. Owen Aldridge

A. Owen Aldridge, professor of French and comparative literature at the University of Illinois, explores
Voltaire's stylistic convention of bringing his characters' idealism in contact with brutal reality through
stark juxtapositions. By contrasting his characters'
optimism with the evils of human society, Voltaire illustrates how far people have degenerated. But the
last scene in *Candide* then raises the question of
whether it is better to live in a world of evil or to remain isolated and inactive in a world of boredom.
Voltaire's answer, as Aldridge points out, has been
the subject of much critical debate.

Unlike *Zadig* and Voltaire's other philosophical tales that
have a protagonist but no other characters, *Candide* has a
roster of personae. In this sense it is closer to a conventional
novel than is [Jonathan Swift's] *Gulliver's Travels*, the literary work which it resembles most and which served as a
partial model. It can even be considered as a parody of the
seventeenth-century *Bildungsroman*, in which moral education is carried on by means of extensive travel in the company of an all-knowing tutor. . . . Candide's mentor is the
perennially cheerful Pangloss, who taught not that all is
right, as did [British poet and philosopher Alexander] Pope
and many other optimists, but that all is for the best in the
best of all possible worlds, an exaggeration of ordinary
deism, and a verbal echo of [the ideas of German scientist
Gottfried Wilhelm] Leibniz. Sex interest is provided by
Cunégonde, the daughter of the castle, whose fatal kiss
causes Candide's first misfortune. Cunégonde is later repeatedly raped or seduced by a series of masters, but Candide himself is never introduced to sexual pleasure. As a re-

Excerpted from A. Owen Aldridge, *Voltaire and the Century of Light.* Copyright © 1975
Princeton University Press. Reprinted with permission from Princeton University
Press.

frain to the empty declamations of Pangloss, Candide repeats with naïve confidence after every scene of horror his
conviction that this is the best of all possible worlds.

The completely opposite point of view is expressed by two
characters who serve as foils to Candide and his mentor:
Jacques, a charitable Anabaptist, expounds the doctrine of
the moral degeneration of man; and Martin, a Manichean,
teaches the supremacy of evil rather than a balance of evil
and good. Both are more often than not spokesmen for
Voltaire. A Venetian nobleman, Pococurante, . . . expresses
literary and dramatic theories exactly parallel to those in
Voltaire's previously published works, even though he cannot be taken as a [characterization] of all of Voltaire's esthetic notions. Even Frederick appears briefly as the king of
the Bulgares, a military conqueror spreading bloodshed and
destruction. The band is completed by a picaresque valet,
Cacambo, from South America; an old woman (daughter of
a pope); a priest, and a prostitute, the latter two living together in apparent bliss but actual torment. These assorted
philosophical symbols and character types have uncanny re-
semblances to flesh and blood creatures.

VOLTAIRE'S SATIRIC METHOD

In *Gulliver's Travels* Swift used many methods of satire to
convey his message of gloom, but Voltaire concentrates on
one only—contrast or ludicrous juxtaposition—developed in
many forms. The basic structure of *Candide* consists of a
naïve, idealistic mind coming into constant contact with opposing realities. Doctrines are refuted by events, not arguments. Candide, among other misadventures, is turned out
of his home; is forcibly impressed into the Bulgarian army;
is brought to the verge of death by being forced to run the
gauntlet; witnesses a bloody battle in which thirty thousand
men are slaughtered; survives a tempest, a shipwreck, and
the famous Lisbon earthquake; and is whipped to insensi-
bility by the Inquisition. During these and scores of other
horrible episodes, he repeats the phrases of Pangloss, that
everything is for the best in the physical and moral realms,
and that nothing could be any otherwise than it is. He per-
sists, as he himself admits, in "the mania of saying all is well
when all is evil." Early in the narrative, a recruiting officer
promises Candide, "Your fortune is made, your glory assured." Immediately he is clapped into irons. At the hands of

the Inquisition, Candide is "preached at, beaten, absolved, and blessed."

Only once in his narrative does Voltaire abandon the technique of exposing the evils of life and of nature by stark realistic portrayal—in a visit to Eldorado. This mythical realm in South America represents the reverse of the world of actuality in both physical and intellectual characteristics. It belongs to the universe of fantasy or science fiction because of its location and natural resources. Hidden in the midst of inaccessible mountains, Eldorado is paved with gold and precious stones, which the inhabitants treat as baubles. From the perspective of society and ideas, Eldorado is a pure Utopia. Its people are completely rational; they can conceive of only one possible religion, deism; they have no priestly class, no prisons, and no law courts, but in their place, they have a palace of science filled with instruments of mathematics and physics. Voltaire, in employing this reversal of perspective—that is, in passing from the exposing of reality to portrayal of the ideal—is following the example of *Gulliver's Travels*, in which we find an identical duality of perspective. Unlike Swift, however, Voltaire reveals that even Utopia is not satisfying to mankind. It is human nature, he affirms, "to enjoy running around, to make oneself to be esteemed by one's peers, and to make a show of what one has seen on one's travels." Voltaire subtly reveals that the perfection in Eldorado is pure exaggeration by pointing out that all of the jokes told by its king are funny. Of all the astonishing features of the land, this is not the least astonishing.

VOLTAIRE EXAMINES HIS TIMES

Throughout his narrative, Voltaire brings into review many scientific, social, and philosophical notions of paramount interest to him and to the age. He glances at [French philosopher Jean-Jacques] Rousseau's doctrine of equality in the state of nature in a chapter on the land of the *oreillons* or ape men, deriving the name of the race from Garcilaso de la Vega's description of *Orejones*, or Indians with big ears. When Candide sees two ape men beating two females of their kind, who respond amorously, Candide is bewildered and curious over why they should take pleasure in the pain inflicted upon them. Later the whole tribe of ape men prepare to eat Candide for dinner, and they are kept from doing so only when they discover that he is not a Jesuit. The existence of cannibalism represented throughout Voltaire's intellectual career one of the major arguments against the doctrine of a universal natural law. The artless Candide concludes that since he has been saved from being devoured merely by the circumstance of not being a Jesuit, the state of pure nature is good.

The evils of institutionalized religion are symbolized by the Jesuits in Paraguay. In their missionary settlement, *los Padres* have everything, the people nothing; the Jesuits consume a delicious luncheon in the shade, the Indians nibble their corn in the heat of the noonday sun.

The common attitude toward suicide, which Voltaire had previously considered in print and in his personal correspondence, he treats in *Candide* as an example of the perversity of human nature. The ridiculous weakness of clinging to one's life is one of the most baneful inclinations, "for there is nothing more stupid than to desire to carry continually a burden which one always wishes to throw to the ground."

Candide takes from Eldorado to Europe a sheep bearing red wool, and the Academy of Bordeaux offers a prize for the best explanation of the causes of this phenomenon. This is a parody of an actual prize offered by this academy in 1741 for the best essay on why the skin of the Negro race is black. True to his prejudices against biological science, Voltaire satirized this inquiry, but he treated with respect a geological query which had previously intrigued him personally, whether the earth was at one time completely covered with water. Candide merely asks Martin his opinion, and the latter says that he has none.

In commenting on the European political scene, Voltaire described six dethroned kings eating together at a cabaret in Venice, each of the kings representing an actual monarch in history who had lost his reigning power. This episode serves to reduce the grandeur associated with royalty and to provide Voltaire with a small measure of revenge for the indignities he had suffered at the hands of Louis XV and Frederick [the Great, king of Prussia].

In one passage, Voltaire repeats the arguments he had previously used to vindicate his *Poem on the Disaster of Lisbon,* particularly the theory that both man and nature have degenerated and that the Christian myth of the fall of man in Eden is closer to the truth than the system of optimism. Through the person of the charitable anabaptist Jacques, Voltaire affirms that men have tended to corrupt nature: they were not born wolves, but have become wolves; god gave them neither cannon nor bayonets, but they forged their weapons in order to destroy. If Jacques is a spokesman for Voltaire himself, and there is good reason for believing that he is, Voltaire almost seems to be vindicating Rousseau's doctrine that society vitiates mankind. He is certainly repudiating the doctrine of the unchanging nature of the universe, which he had previously expounded in his *Discourse on the Changes which Have Occurred on Our Globe.* In a sense, Rousseau was correct in insisting that Candide was an answer to his letter in which he had affirmed that "providence is always right, according to the pious, and always wrong, according to the philosopher." In *Candide*, Pangloss and Martin . . . think exactly alike concerning the presence of suffering in the world; they disagree only in the interpretation of the evidence. Pangloss recognizes only good; the other, only evil. From this prospect, Pangloss represents Rousseau and Martin, Voltaire. At the end of the story, Voltaire succeeds in bringing their opposing perspectives toward a common plane: the question then to be resolved is no longer whether all is right, but whether the other people whom Candide meets on his travels are more to be pitied than he. It is significant to note . . . that there is no philosophical discussion in the story which is not abruptly cut short and left hanging in the air. In his conclusion Voltaire also refuses "to accept an abstract, philosophical answer to the long debate over Optimism."

THE PUZZLING CONCLUSION

In his final chapter, Voltaire completely abandons the metaphysical speculation he had shared with other poets and philosophers in order to present notions typical of himself alone. Much of the universal popularity of *Candide*, therefore, is due to this final chapter. Here all the characters are brought together in the same locale—a house in the country. This circumstance, together with the constant disappearances and mysterious reappearances of the main characters throughout the narrative, suggests that *Candide* is a parody of the structure of romantic fiction of the time as well as an intellectual satire. Voltaire elsewhere ridiculed Calprenède's seventeenth-century method of constructing a novel upon a heap of improbable adventures brought into the semblance of order by the interrogation of an old man or a nurse. He may also have had in mind the more modern "roman polisson," [smutty novel] or even novels such as *Manon Lescaut* of the abbé Prévost.

In the concluding section the old woman, after summarizing the worst mishaps and physical agonies suffered by the entire band, wants to know which is worse, "to experience all the miseries which all of us have experienced, or to stay here and do nothing." "It is a great question," says Candide. The doctrine of boredom, one of Voltaire's most characteristic, is expressed several times in his works. "Our greatest enemy is boredom," he affirmed in a poem dedicated to Mme Denis in 1748; "one cannot live with company, or without it" [*A Mme Denis, nièce de l'auteur, La Vie de Paris et de Versailles*]. In his early *Philosophical Letters*, however, he had considered resentment at the tedium of life to be one of the salutary characteristics of man. Contrary to [French philosopher Blaise] Pascal, who had described the state of mankind as wretched because man can be discontented without any external cause for his dissatisfaction, Voltaire insisted that "on the contrary man is fortunate on this point, and we have an obligation to the author of nature to the degree that he has attached ennui to inaction in order thus to compel us to be useful to our neighbor and to our selves." In his *Philosophical Letters* Voltaire looks at boredom in the optimistic spirit of Pangloss; in *Candide* Voltaire does not consider ennui a blessing, but he offers a means of escape—his famous conclusion, "we must cultivate our garden."

This conclusion—apparently clear and simple—has puzzled critics and ordinary readers ever since the publication of *Candide*. What exactly does it mean? One might assume that Voltaire is suggesting husbandry as a remedy for boredom. This is borne out by a letter from Voltaire to Mme Denis in 1753 in which he described gardening as "an occupation which destroys boredom." In the same month, while deploring "the idleness of the country," he remarked, "it is better to dig in the ground than to suffer boredom." In a letter to Cideville written during the composition of *Candide*, however, he seemed to give a contrary interpretation, affirming that "retirement is good only with good company" and that the secret of happiness is found neither in the fields, the court, nor the city.

Whether or not the cultivation of one's garden is necessarily linked to the dispelling of boredom, we still need to interpret the meaning of Voltaire's famous conclusion. It might refer simply to hedonism, as in the phrase "The Gardens of Epicurus," which he had used in an ode describing his arrival at Les Délices. The injunction to horticulture might be alluding to the antiquity and respectability in the humanistic tradition of the concept of orderly cultivation. As Bacon had previously said in reference to Eden, "God almighty first planted a garden." In this sense, Voltaire's prescription of cultivation seems to rebuke Rousseau's emphasis on wild nature. Or Voltaire might simply have wished to suggest abandoning activities of the world in favor of personal ease—activities of either an egocentric or a philanthropic nature, both of which occasionally obtruded on his personal composure. The eighteenth-century Russian novelist Karamzin believed that Voltaire had in mind respite from the weariness of metaphysical speculation. One could add to Candide's phrase, according to Karamzin, "Let us love our family, relations, and friends, and leave the rest to the will of destiny." Voltaire may even have been thinking of himself as a writer and social critic, and conceived of his garden as a retreat from the attacks of his enemies. In a fragment of unknown date published in his *Notebooks,* he denounced the secret rage with which envy pursues all real talents, and concluded that minds kindred to his should follow the example "of the author of La Henriade and cultivate his talents in a desert." Some critics have assumed that Candide's final words reflect a faith in the future, and some have even maintained that they foreshadow the political doctrine of anarchism, each man going his own way. . . .

The obvious meaning of Candide's words is, of course, the literal one, not only that gardening dispels boredom, but that it produces positive good. There are many passages in Voltaire's correspondence to confirm this interpretation, beginning with [English statesman Henry St. John, Viscount] Bolingbroke's letter in 1724 setting forth a parallel between cultivating one's character and one's garden. Soon after taking up residence at Les Délices, Voltaire wrote to Robert Tronchin, to whom the estate would revert after Voltaire's death, "I am concerned only with cultivating your garden in peace." Somewhat later he wrote to [French encyclopedist Denis] Diderot, the "labors of the country seem to belong to philosophy. The good experiments of physics are those of the cultivation of the land." In the year following the publication of *Candide,* Frederick commended Voltaire on his wisdom in following the counsel to cultivate his garden. Frederick seemed to suggest that Voltaire was reflecting his own experience and contentment at Les Délices. Soon after taking up his residence there, Voltaire exulted: "Happy is he who lives in his own property with his nieces, his books, his garden, his vines, his horses, his cows, his eagle, his fox and his rabbits, which rub their noses with their paws. I have all of that and the Alps to boot which create an admirable effect. I much prefer to lecture my gardeners than to play courtier to kings." In similar mood he observed to Mme Du Deffand that there is only one pleasure to be preferred to literary ones, and that is "seeing vast prairies turn green and beautiful crops grow." If Candide's words are to be taken literally, they foreshadow the tribute of Thomas Jefferson, "Those who labour in the earth are the chosen people of God, whose breasts he has made his peculiar deposit for substantial and genuine virtue." This is as close to primitivism as Voltaire ever came.

CHRONOLOGY

1694

Born François-Marie Arouet to middle-class parents, Marie-Marguerite Daumard and François Arouet, in Paris on November 21.

1701

Mother dies.

1704

Begins studies at Louis-le-Grand, a Jesuit school in Paris.

1710

Gottfried Wilhelm Leibniz publishes *Theodicy*.

1711

Leaves school; joins Society of the Temple.

1713

In Holland as secretary to French ambassador; affair with Pimpette; sent home by ambassador.

1714

Begins studying law in Paris, making little progress in law but much in writing.

1716

Forced exile at Sully-sur-Loire because of "distasteful" works.

1717

Imprisoned in Bastille for eleven months; assumes name Voltaire.

1718

Released from prison; play *Oedipus* is produced in Paris.

1720

Play *Artemire* opens and fails.

1722

Father dies; pensioned by the king; writes *The Epistle to Urania.*

1723

Publishes *The League,* the first version of *The Henriade;* gets smallpox; regent dies and Louis XV becomes king.

1725

Pensioned by new queen; quarrel with Chevalier de Rohan-Chabot.

1726

Imprisoned again in the Bastille for challenging de Rohan-Chabot to duel; is exiled to England; is received by the king of England; meets English literary figures, including Jonathan Swift and Alexander Pope; publishes *Essay on Epic Poetry.*

1728

The Henriade is published in England and dedicated to the English queen.

1729

Returns to France.

1730

Tragedy *Brutus* is produced; writes poem "The Death of Mademoiselle Lecouvreur."

1731

History of Charles XII, King of Sweden is published; in it he urges kings to strive for peace.

1732

Zaire is produced in Paris.

1733

The Temple of Taste; Pope's *An Essay on Man* is published in England.

1734

Publication of *Philosophical Letters* (also called *Letters on the English Nation*), which causes outrage in France; flees with Emilie du Châtelet to Cirey; writes *Treatise on Metaphysics* (unpublished).

1735

Return to Paris; *The Death of Caesar* is produced.

1736

Alzire is successful in Paris; begins correspondence with Prince Frederick; goes to Holland; writes *The Man of the World.*

1738

Publishes *Elements of Newton's Philosophy* and *Discourse in Verse on Man.*

1740

First meeting with Frederick at Cleves.

1742

Mahomet is produced in Paris; creates controversy and closes.

1743

Mérope is successful in Paris.

1745

Is appointed royal historiographer to Louis XV; death of his brother; writes *The Temple of Glory.*

1746

Is elected to the French Academy.

1747

Publishes *Zadig,* a philosophical tale; flees from court with du Châtelet to Sceaux; visits court of King Stanislaus at Lunéville.

1749

Death of Emilie du Châtelet.

1750

Orestes is published; goes to live in Potsdam in court of Frederick the Great.

1751

The Age of Louis XIV is published.

1752

Publishes *Micromégas,* a philosophical novel.

1753

Leaves Prussia; Frederick has him arrested with his niece at

Frankfurt. His baggage is searched for copies of a book Voltaire published (without Frederick's permission) in which the writer attacked the president of Prussia's Academy of Science.

1754

Arrives in Geneva.

1755

Buys 'Les Délices,' an estate in Geneva; Lisbon earthquake kills thirty thousand; writes *Poem on the Lisbon Earthquake.*

1757

Quarrels with Genevan authorities over opposition to theatrical performances at Les Délices; resumes correspondence with Frederick the Great.

1758

Arranges to buy estate at Ferney in France near Geneva.

1759

Moves to Ferney; *Candide* is published.

1761

Erects church at Ferney.

1762

Jean Calas is executed; writes *Sermon of the Fifty.*

1763

The Age of Louis XV is published; writes *Treatise on Tolerance* in defense of Jean Calas.

1764

Publishes *Philosophical Dictionary,* which sets forth the main ideas of rationalism.

1765

Calas's name is cleared; Voltaire defends the Sirven family.

1766

Execution of Chevalier de la Barre, a young boy accused of sacrilege; writes *The Ignorant Philosopher* and *Account of the Death of the Chevalier de la Barre* (which posthumously cleared his name).

1767

The *Ingenu* is published.

1771

Sirven is cleared.

1774

Louis XV dies; Louis XVI takes throne.

1778

Voltaire returns to Paris; sees *Irene* performed; dies May 30.

FOR FURTHER RESEARCH

ABOUT VOLTAIRE

A. Owen Aldridge, *Voltaire and the Century of Light*. Princeton, NJ: Princeton University Press, 1975.

Georg Brandes, *Voltaire*. 2 vols. Trans. Otto Kruger and Pierce Butler. New York: Frederick Ungar, 1964.

Peter Gay, *Voltaire's Politics: The Poet as a Realist*. Princeton, NJ: Princeton University Press, 1959.

Gustav Lanson, *Voltaire*. Trans. Robert A. Wagoner. New York: John Wiley and Sons, 1966.

Haydn Mason, *Voltaire*. New York: St. Martin's, 1975.

Peyton Richter and Ilona Ricardo, *Voltaire*. Boston: Twayne, 1980.

S.G. Tallentyre, *The Life of Voltaire*. New York: Loring and Mussey, n.d.

Victor Thaddeus, *Voltaire: Genius of Mockery*. New York: Brentano's, 1928.

Ira O. Wade, *The Intellectual Development of Voltaire*. Princeton, NJ: Princeton University Press, 1969.

CRITICAL WORKS ON *CANDIDE*

W.H. Barber, *Voltaire: "Candide."* London: Arnold, 1960.

C.J. Betts, "On the Beginning and Ending of *Candide.*" *Modern Language Review*, vol. 80, April 1985.

William F. Bottiglia, ed., *Voltaire: A Collection of Critical Essays*. Englewood Cliffs, NJ: Prentice Hall, 1968.

Milton P. Foster, ed., *Voltaire's "Candide" and the Critics*. Belmont, CA: Wadsworth, 1962.

Roger Pearson, *The Fables of Reason: A Study of Voltaire's "Contes Philosophiques."* Oxford: Clarendon, 1993.

Ira O. Wade, *Voltaire and "Candide": A Study in the Fusion of History, Art, and Philosophy*. Princeton, NJ: Princeton University Press, 1959.

Renee Waldinger, ed., *Approaches to Teaching Voltaire's "Candide."* New York: Modern Language Association of America, 1987.

ABOUT VOLTAIRE'S TIME

Ernst Cassirer, *The Philosophy of the Enlightenment.* Trans. Fritz C.A. Koelin and James P. Pettegrove. Princeton, NJ: Princeton University Press, 1951.

Harold Nicolson, *The Age of Reason.* Garden City, NY: Doubleday, 1960.

George Stade, ed., *European Writers: The Age of Reason and the Enlightenment.* 4 vols. New York: Charles Scribner's Sons, 1984.

VERSIONS OF *CANDIDE*

Peter Gay, ed. and trans., *Candide.* Bilingual ed. New York: St. Martin's, 1963.

Voltaire, *Candide.* Trans. unknown. New York: Dover, 1991.

David Williams, ed., and trans. *Candide.* London: Grant and Cutler, 1997.

INDEX

Adams, Robert, 118, 145, 146
Aethiopica (Heliodorus), 106
Age of Louis XIV, The, 18
Aldridge, A. Owen, 151
Alzire, 18
Anatomy of Criticism (Frye),
  107
Anti-Machiavelli (Frederick
  II), 18
Arouet, François (Voltaire's
  father), 13
Arouet, François-Marie. *See*
  Voltaire
Arouet, Marguerite-
  Catherine (Voltaire's sister),
  15
  death of, 17
Artemire, 16

Babouc, 50
Barth, John, 113, 117
Bernstein, Leonard, 51
Besterman, Theodore, 11
Betts, C.J., 136
Bildungsroman, 151
  see also quest literature
black humor
  and satire, similarities,
    112–15
  suicide as topic of, 116–17
Bottiglia, William F., 65, 81,
  95, 141–43

Breton, Andre, 112
burlesque
  Candide as, 105–106, 113

Calas, Jean, 23
Camus, Albert, 37
Candide
  as black humor, 112–20
  conclusion of
    contrasting speeches at,
      86
    and death of hope, 119–20
    emphasis on gender
      equality in, 139–40
    hope for moral
      improvement in, 46
  is pessimistic view of
    human condition, 112
  meaning of, 87, 156
  dialectics of, 121–22
  influences on, 20–21
  narration of, 125–26
  plot of, 25–31, 113
    expectation-frustration
      rhythm in, 121–22
  as prototype of realistic
    fiction, 63
  scope of, 50, 52
  as view of degenerate man,
    151–58
  women's equality in,
    129–40

writing of, 22–23
Candide (Bernstein), 51
Candy (Southern), 113
Castle of Thunder-ten-
  tronckh
  as fool's paradise, 36
  as microcosm of Old
    Régime, 140
Catch-22 (Heller), 115
Cat's Cradle (Vonnegut), 119
Céline, Louis-Ferdinand, 114
Cervantes, Miguel de, 55
characters, 25
  are driven by animal
    appetites, 108–109
  Cacambo, 72–73, 117, 124
    in Eldorado, 59–60
  Candide
    as Adam figure, 36, 89,
      140
    definition of optimism, 39
    in Eldorado, 59–60, 74–75
    infantile nature of, 124,
      131
    intellectual growth of, 35,
      36, 79, 80, 96
    as ironic hero, 144
    moral improvement of, 46
    and narrative technique,
      125–26
    relationship with
      Cunégonde, 133–34
    Voltaire's detachment
      from, 143
  Cunégonde, 34, 37, 117,
    123, 124
    Candide's relationship
      with, 133–34
    as Eve figure, 36, 89, 140
    intellectual maturation of,
      35–36, 137–38
    role of, in Candide's
      garden, 84, 148
    as symbol of eternal

woman, 48
    and theme of hope, 41
  Giroflée, 137
    improvement in lot of, 148
    role of, in Candide's
      garden, 84
  James (Jacques) the
    Anabaptist, 41, 149–50,
    154
    as spokesman for Voltaire,
      155
  Martin, 81, 117
    on importance of money,
      145
    Manicheanism of, 34, 35
    as mentor of Candide,
      43–44
    pessimistic views of, 42
    as representative of
      Voltaire, 155
    role of, in Candide's
      garden, 84
  Old Woman (La Vielle), 38,
    40–41, 122, 148
    dilemma in choosing life
      over suicide, 109, 116–17
    role of, in Candide's self-
      realization, 134–35
    strength in character of,
      130–31
  Pangloss, 40, 124
    defense of optimism by,
      54
    encounter with Paquette,
      136
    as personification of
      stupidity and evil, 147
    ridicule of, 34
    role of, in Candide's
      garden, 84
  Paquette
    improvement in lot of, 148
    role of, in Candide's
      garden, 84

as sympathetic character, 132, 136
Pococurante, 38, 53–54, 132–33
as reflection of reader's needs, 121–27
use of, to disprove optimism, 39–46
Vanderdendur, 41, 124
Châtelet, Emilie du, 18, 130
Cherpak, Clifton, 11, 105
chivalric romance
    Candide as spoof of, 36
    influence on *Candide*, 34
Clarke, Samuel, 17
comedy
    in accumulated ordeals, 34
    low, in mockery of philosophical pretensions, 105–11
    see also satire
Crocker, Lester, 48

Dalnekoff, Donna Isaacs, 64
Daumard, Marie-Marguerite (Voltaire's mother), 13
Diderot, Denis, 157
Discourses in Verse of Man, 18
Don Quixote (Cervantes), 55, 63
Dunoyer, Olympe (Pimpette), 14

Eden, garden of, 58
    Candide as parody of, 48
    Westphalian garden as, 88–90
Eldorado, 36–37
    Candide's departure from, 70–71, 79–80
    reasons for, 48, 93
    and Candide's garden, 82, 83

discontinuity between, 95–96
description of, 73–74
distinction from Edenic garden, 92
and garden symbolism, 59–61
government institutions in, 68–69, 76–78
passage into, 90–92
and problem of isolation, 61–63
religion in, 76, 92–93
as reverse of actual world, 153
science in, 78–79
as Utopia, 64–67, 72
Eliade, Miscea, 90
enlightened monarchy, 19
Enlightenment: An Interpretation, The (Gay), 141
Epistle to Urania, 17
Essai sur les moeurs, 65
Essay on Man (Pope), 21, 39, 42–43
existential literature, 120

Ferney, 21–22
Floating Opera (Barth), 117
France, Anatole, 55
Franklin, Benjamin, 23
Frederick II "the Great," 18–19, 158
    King of Bulgars as parody of, 103
Friedman, Bruce Jay, 114
Frye, Northrop, 107, 109

gardens
    in art and literature, 57
    Cacambo's, 82, 95
    Candide's
        and Eldorado, 82, 83

gender equality in, 138–40
social harmony of, 95–96
comparison of, 82–83
cultivation of
as best way to live in
absurd world, 110–11
critical interpretation of,
142
as process, 62–63
and progression to
community, 83–85
the Turk's, 44, 82–83
and social responsibility,
49
Voltaire's conception of, 87
Westphalian, as Edenic,
88–90
Gay, Peter, 141, 142
Genette, Gerard, 125
Gravity's Rainbow
(Pynchon), 114, 118
Gulliver's Travels (Swift),
112, 151, 153

Hall, Evelyn, 20
Havens, George R., 12, 98
Hazlitt, William, 100
Heliodorus, 106
Heller, Joseph, 115
Henriade, The, 16
Henry, Patrick, 12, 88
*Histoire des voyages de
Scarmentado,* 39
History of Charles XII, 17

illogical absurdities
grammatical union of,
102–103
imagery
light, in Eldorado, 91
Inquisition, 52, 138
internal focus, 125
Irene, 23
irony

in character of Candide,
144
in depiction of levels of
civilization, 94
as form of satire in
Candide, 98–104
in individual helplessness,
83
in Pangloss's defense of
optimism, 54
in treatment of human
foibles, 98

"J'ai vu," 15
Jefferson, Thomas, 158
Jung, Carl, 96

Kant, Immanuel, 89
Kusch, Manfred, 57

Leibniz, Gottfried Wilhelm,
22, 33, 38, 39, 47, 151
"pre-established harmony"
idea, 113
satire on cause-and-effect
reasoning of, 108
leitmotivs
gender equality, 139
Lettres persanes
(Montesquieu), 76
L'ingénu, 109–10, 121
Lisbon earthquake, 20–21
Locke, John, 17, 36
Louis XIV, 15
Louis XV, 15
low comedy
in mockery of
philosophical pretensions,
105–11

Manicheanism, 29, 34
Man of the World, The, 18
Manon Lescaut (Prévost),
156

Mason, Haydn, 39
Micromégas, 50
Mignon, Abbé, 23
"Modernity of *Candide,* The"
  (Henry), 12
Mohammed, 18
monarchy
  in Eldorado, 37, 77
  enlightened, 19
  Voltaire's comment on, 154
Montesquieu, 75

narration, 125–26
nature
  as benevolent, in Eldorado,
    73

Oedipus, 16
Olderman, Raymond, 114
optimism, philosophy of, 21
  Candide as satire of, 33
    humanitarian goals
      underlying, 47–55
  Candide's rejection of, 71
  possibility for, 37–38
  Voltaire's view of, 22, 81–82
Orellions, 73, 117, 123, 153

parody
  on book of Genesis, 89
  of Garden of Eden and
    original sin, 48
  of quest literature, 90
  on romantic fiction, 155
  as strategy of black
    humorists, 113
Pascal, Blaise, 17–18, 156
Pearson, Roger, 33
Philip, duke of Orleans, 15
"Philippics, The," 16
Philosophical Letters, 17
picaresque literature, 113
Pimpette (Olympe Dunoyer),
  14

plot
  organization of, as
    expectation and
    frustration, 121–22
  summary of, 25–31
*Poem on the Disaster in
  Lisbon,* 21, 107, 154
Pomeau, René, 82, 86, 95
Pope, Alexander, 17, 21, 22,
  33, 38, 42–43, 47, 151
Porter, Andrew, 51
Pratt, Alan R., 112
Pynchon, Thomas, 114

quest literature
  Candide as parody of, 90
Quintessence, 14

Rabelais, François, 65
reduction
  Voltaire's use of, 147–50
Reed, Gail S., 121, 131
religion
  in Eldorado, 76, 92–93
  Jesuits as symbols of evils
    of, 154
  as target of satire, 52
ridicule
  Voltaire's use of, 101
Rohan-Chabot, chevalier de,
  16
romance
  Candide as burlesque of,
    106, 113
  chivalric
    Candide as spoof of, 36
    influence on *Candide,* 34
Rousseau, Jean-Jacques, 21,
  47, 54, 78, 153
  Pangloss as representative
    of, 155

Sareil, Jean, 95
Sartre, Jean-Paul, 41

satire, 106–107
  and black humor,
    similarities, 112–15
  on human behavior, 108
  on human notions of
    wealth, 66–67
  irony as form of, 98–104
  low norm, 109, 110–11
  of optimism, 33
  of philosophical systems,
    107
  of religion, 52, 67–68
  of social institutions, 101
  targets of, 52–54
  use of reduction in, 147
  Voltaire's method of,
    152–53
Satyricon (Petronius), 106
Scherr, Arthur, 129
Schulz, Max, 117
Seven Years' War, 99, 114
Slaughterhouse Five
  (Vonnegut), 114–15
Sot-Weed Factor, The (Barth),
  113
Southern, Terry, 113
St. John, Henry, 157
stylistic devices
  exaggeration, 104
  grammatical union of
    illogical absurdities,
    102–103
  intentional
    understatement, 102
  juxtaposition, 115–16, 152
  nonsequitur, 104–105, 115
  repetition, 104
suicide, 109, 154
  as topic of black humor,
    116–17
Swift, Jonathan, 112, 153
symbolism
  in act of climbing, 91
  in descent from Eldorado,

94
  the garden, 57–58
  the river, 58–59

Tatius, Achilles, 106
Temple of Taste, 17
themes
  avoidance of vice, 145–46
  connection between
    stupidity and evil, 146–47
  desire to impose order on
    experience, 34
  education and
    enlightenment, 34, 35–36
  freedom of action, 83
  friendship and shared
    feelings/experiences, 75
  hope, in face of adversity,
    41
  horror of evil vs. zest for
    life, 40
  irrelevance of
    philosophical systems,
    107
  problem of boredom, 45,
    49, 79, 118, 145
  relativism, 116–18
  state of pure nature, 153–54
  superiority of productivity,
    85, 141
  vanity and human
    behavior, 107
  work ethic of modern
    capitalism, 137
Theodicy (Leibnitz), 39
"Thoughts on Pascal," 17
Topazio, Virgil W., 47
Torrey, Norman L., 81, 82,
  142
Tronchin, Robert, 157

understatement, 102
Utopia
  characteristics of, 65, 66

Van Doren, Mark, 144
Voltaire (François-Marie
    Arouet)
    birth and childhood of,
        13–14
    death of, 23
    in England, 17
    exiles of, 15, 16
    famous observations of, 78
    at Ferney, 21–22
    in Frederick's court, 19–20
    in Geneva, 20
    Martin as representative of,
        155
    style and ironic method of,
        101–104
    view on prose fiction, 111
    and women, 129–30
*Voltaire's "Candide" and the
    Critics* (Foster), 42–43, 100
Vonnegut, Kurt, 115
V (Pynchon), 118

Wallace, Ronald, 119
war, 52
    satire of, 99–101

wealth
    Candide as satire on
        human notions of, 66–67
    symbols of, in Eldorado vs.
        outside world, 74
Weightman, J.G., 40
Williams, David, 72
Wolper, Roy S., 141
women
    characters, strength of,
        130–32
    Cunégonde as symbol of,
        48
    equality of, Candide's
        garden, 138–40
    role in Candide's self-
        realization, 134–36
    as target of satire, 53
    Voltaire's disgust with
        treatment of, 132–33
    in Voltaire's life, 129–30
Wordsworth, William, 100

Zadig, 50, 109–10, 121, 151
Zaire, 17